www.ingramcontent.com/pod-product-compliance
Lightning Source LLC
Chambersburg PA
CBHW062058290426

44110CB00022B/2633

Themes of the Passover Haggadah

By David Silberman

Dedicated to my wife, **Dina**.

שאין ברכה מצויה בתוך ביתו של אדם אלא בשביל אשתו
There is no blessing in a man's house except for his wife.

Talmud Baba Metzia 59a

And dedicated to my children

Nathan

Debora

Esther and Eyal Shavitzky
and their daughters,
Abigail & Gabrielle

for all the questions they have asked and continue to ask.
May Pesach be as memorable for their children
as it has been for me.

Nissan 5774, April 2014

Copyright 2014 by David M. Silberman

All rights reserved un International and Pan-American Copyright Conventions

Published in the United States by HaggadahPublishing.com

v

Library of Congress Control Number: 2014903705

ISBN–13: 978-0615974118

Design by Emuna Carmel

סֵדֶר בְּדִיקַת חָמֵץ

בָּרוּךְ אַתָּה יְיָ אֱלֹהֵינוּ מֶלֶךְ הָעוֹלָם
אֲשֶׁר קִדְּשָׁנוּ בְּמִצְוֹתָיו וְצִוָּנוּ עַל בִּעוּר חָמֵץ.

כָּל חֲמִירָא וַחֲמִיעָא דְּאִכָּא בִרְשׁוּתִי,
דְּלָא חֲמִתֵּהּ וּדְלָא בִעַרְתֵּהּ וּדְלָא יְדַעְנָא לֵיהּ,
לִבְטִיל וְלֶהֱוֵי הֶפְקֵר כְּעַפְרָא דְאַרְעָא.

סֵדֶר שְׂרֵפַת חָמֵץ

כָּל חֲמִירָא וַחֲמִיעָא דְּאִכָּא בִרְשׁוּתִי,
דַּחֲזִיתֵּהּ וּדְלָא חֲזִיתֵּהּ, דַּחֲמִיתֵּהּ וּדְלָא חֲמִתֵּהּ,
דְּדִבְעַרְתֵּהּ וּדְלָא בִעַרְתֵּהּ, לִבָּטֵל וְלֶהֱוֵי הֶפְקֵר כְּעַפְרָא דְאַרְעָא.

Searching for Chametz

On the night before Passover, the fourteenth of Nisan, a search for leavened products is done in ones house. Traditionally this search is done by candlelight. Prior to beginning the search the following blessing is said:

Blessed are You, Hashem our God, King of the Universe, Who has made us holy with His commandments and commanded us about the eradication of chametz.

After completing the search the following declaration is said aloud:

Any type of leavened product that is in my possession, that I have not found and have not removed and do not know about, is hereby nullified and made ownerless like the dust of the earth.

Burning the Chametz

On the morning of the fourteenth of Nisan, the leavened products found the night before and those products not sold are burned. The burning of these leavened products should be accomplished an hour before midday and the following recited:

Any type of leavened product in my possession, whether I have seen it or I have not seen it, whether I have found it or not found it, removed it or not removed it, is hereby nullified and made ownerless like the dust of the earth.

עֵרוּב תַּבְשִׁילִין

בָּרוּךְ אַתָּה יְיָ אֱלֹהֵינוּ מֶלֶךְ הָעוֹלָם
אֲשֶׁר קִדְּשָׁנוּ בְּמִצְוֹתָיו וְצִוָּנוּ עַל מִצְוַת עֵרוּב.

בַּהֲדֵין עֵרוּבָא יְהֵא שָׁרֵי לָנָא לְמֵיפָא וּלְבַשָּׁלָא וּלְאַטְמַנָא וּלְאַדְלָקָא שְׁרָגָא, וּלְמֶעֱבַד כָּל צָרְכָנָא, מִיּוֹמָא טָבָא לְשַׁבַּתָּא, לָנוּ וּלְכָל יִשְׂרָאֵל הַדָּרִים בָּעִיר הַזֹּאת.

סֵדֶר הַדְלָקַת נֵרוֹת

בָּרוּךְ אַתָּה יְיָ, אֱלֹהֵינוּ מֶלֶךְ הָעוֹלָם, אֲשֶׁר קִדְּשָׁנוּ בְּמִצְוֹתָיו, וְצִוָּנוּ לְהַדְלִיק נֵר שֶׁל (בשבת: שֶׁל שַׁבָּת וְשֶׁל) יוֹם טוֹב.

בָּרוּךְ אַתָּה יְיָ, אֱלֹהֵינוּ מֶלֶךְ הָעוֹלָם, שֶׁהֶחֱיָנוּ וְקִיְּמָנוּ וְהִגִּיעָנוּ לַזְּמַן הַזֶּה.

Eruv Tavshilin

When the first days of Pesach fall on Thursday and Friday an Eruv Tavshilin needs to be made to allow one to cook and prepare food on Yom Tov for the Shabbat. The Eruv Tavshilin is made on Wednesday. One should take some matzah and another cooked food and set them aside to be eaten on Shabbat. The following declaration is said:

**Blessed are You, Hashem, our God, King of the universe,
Who has made us holy with His commandments
and commanded us about the mitzvah of Eruv.**

With this Eruv, may we and all the Jews of this town be permitted to bake, cook, put food on the fire, light candles, and do all that we need to, on Yom Tov for the following Shabbat.

Blessing Over the Candles

Blessed are You, Hashem, our God, King of the Universe, Who has sanctified us with His commandments and has commanded us to kindle the light of (Sabbath and of) the Festival.

Blessed are You, Hashem, our God, King of the Universe, Who has kept us alive, sustained us, and brought us to this season.

	זרוע Shank Bone
ביצה Egg	

מרור
Bitter Herbs

כרפס
Green Vegetable

חרוסת
Charoset

חזרת
Bitter Herbs

Introduction

The Haggadah is an anthology of ancient Jewish texts that include passages from the Bible, the Mishna (third century CE), the Talmud (sixth century CE), the Midrash, and later additions from the Middle Ages. The predominate custom, as presented in numerous Haggadahs (there are over two thousand editions) is to analyze, at times in great detail, every word, every sentence and every paragraph. Since the text itself is a disparate collection of various excerpts, overall messages and topics are blurred. As a result, the Seder participant can get lost in the details and fail to grasp the some of the larger issues. Just what are the take home messages?

With an analysis of the Haggadah and keeping in mind the broader Exodus narrative, multiple themes can be identified. It is the purpose of this Haggadah to identify these themes and present them with an emphasis on one theme per reading of the text. In this manner, the topic at hand can be discussed and analyzed within the framework of the traditional Seder and hopefully remembered and internalized.

The themes are listed below and are color-coded. It is suggested that each Seder participant take turns to read different passages as you progress through the Haggadah. Some selections are longer than others and more than one person can share reading the longer ones. This should assist in focusing the attention of the group and lend itself to greater participation and discussion. There is no specific order of the themes; each one stands on its own.

Themes by color:

- Freedom
- Contemporary: the Haggadah is a Story of Modern Times
- Family and Community
- Gratitude
- Redemption
- Israel

קַדֵּשׁ

כוס ראשונה

מוזגים כוס יין לקידוש, וכן מוזגים כוסות לכל המסובים בַּסֵדֶר. כוס הקידוש היא הראשונה מארבע הכוסות, ויש דורשים כי מכוונת היא כנגד 'לשון ראשונה' מ'ארבע לשונות' של גאולת מצרים, ככתוב "והוצאתי אתכם מתחת סבלות מצרים". (שמות ו' ו')

Introduction to the Theme of Freedom

The Haggadah relates "in every generation, a Jew is obligated to see him or herself as having been personally liberated from Egypt." We make an attempt to symbolically relive the Exodus from Egypt by tasting salt water reminiscent of tears, eating bitter herbs to remind us of bitter times, and eating the bread that slaves might have eaten. Four cups of wine are drunk to symbolize various aspects of liberation, all the while reclining as wealthy free individuals. But what relevance does this concept of freedom from ancient slavery have for us today- as individuals and as a community?

The Kiddush over wine, about to be recited, describes this holiday as *chag cheirutainu*, the festival of freedom. This is the theme for tonight's Seder. Freedom: what it means, and the responsibilities and limitations that might accompany it.

While we may not be incarcerated, or find ourselves at the whims of an evil despotic ruler, we are nonetheless servants. This, too, will be explored.

Let us begin.

Introduction to the Theme of Redemption

One of the most common descriptions of the Exodus experience is that God "redeemed" the Jewish people. גאל is the word used and is found throughout the Tanach and prayer books – a most common citation and usually defined as " to be redeemed."

Kadesh

The First Cup

Pour the cup of wine for the Kiddush and similarly pour wine for all the participants of the Seder. The cup of wine for the Kiddush is the first of the four cups of wine and there are those that explain the four cups of wine correspond to the four different expressions of redemption from Egypt as it is written "And I took you out of slavery from Egypt" Exodus 6:6.

What does it mean to be redeemed?

Even Shushan, a biblical dictionary, offers four definitions based on the contextual use of the word גאל (prounounced ga'al):

1. To set free, to save, to release from hardship
2. To pay the value of an item that was held as a deposit
3. To release a woman from a Leverite marriage
4. To restore a forgotten item.

    A word similar in pronunciation to ga'al, perhaps the cognate of גאל and that is געל, (the middle letter changes from א to ע.) The word sounds basically the same but means to spurn, reject or spit out. In order to do any of these, one has to have evaluated the substance or situation from a position of neutrality or even affection, and changed one's opinion to that of rejection.

    I submit that all of the above definitions can be understood by one word and that word is *transformation*. All of the above examples involve a change in status from unfree to free, to encumbrance to available, from out of use to a restored condition, from one level of spiritual existence to another.

    This new use of the term, transformation, revolutionizes one's understanding of the Passover experience as it describes not only the transformation of a group of enslaved people to a free society, but also describes the transformation of an individual mentality from un-free to free. Finally, since the word ga'al is commonly found in our daily prayer book it personalizes our relationship with God since we can read it now as God transforms Israel, God transforms us.

Introduction to the Theme of Israel

Aliya. Ascension. The emigration from a land outside Israel to the land of Israel. Modern history has chronicled the migration of Jews to Israel from the hardships faced in Arab land, from the oppression in the Soviet Union, and before that from ashes of the Holocaust. Jewish migration to Israel has an ancient history beginning only years after the original expulsion in 586 BCE and reasons for returning have included ideology, economy and refuge. The exodus from Egypt represents the first mass Aliya. As the ancient Hebrews left Egypt to physically escape a life of slavery, they ultimately coalesced into a more unified nation via the Revelation at Mount Sinai. Their story of risks taken, oppression, hardships of a long journey culminates in their arrival, home again, in Israel. Their story has been told and relived countless times. Tonight we will examine the presence of Israel in the Haggadah and the exodus narrative.

Introduction to the Theme of Contemporary Nature of the Haggadah

The Haggadah is an anthology of ancient Jewish texts that date from before the first century of the Common Era to medieval times. Multiple themes can be discerned within the Haggadah itself, but is the text and story described therein a contemporary story or only "ancient history"?

A glance at modern history will reveal that the story of the "Exodus" has reoccurred multiple times. There are numerous examples where individuals and groups, small and large in number gained their freedom from physical imprisonment as well as political oppression. During the height of the Second World War, large areas of Europe, Asia, and North Africa were conquered by invading armies, in effect subjugating and enslaving the populations of multiple countries and peoples. The defeat of the occupying forces was a liberating experience for untold millions of people, but not for all. In Eastern Europe, the Nazis were displaced by a new oppressive force – the Soviet Union. The Soviet block eventually was defeated, largely from social and economic changes, again liberating millions from what was a controlling, totalitarian regime. In our very day, borders are being redrawn as ethnic enclaves and commonality of interests are moving populations and new countries are being formed.

The contemporary voice of the Haggadah will be presented It will illustrate that the Seder ceremony and the holiday of Passover speaks to us all here today as much as it has inspired those in the past who were without freedom.

Introduction to the Theme of Family and Community

It has been observed that of all the holidays in the Jewish calendar, The most widely observed holiday in the Jewish calendar is the holiday of Passover. What is it about the Seder night that has such an attraction? Perhaps it is the emphasis on family and community. Pesach highlights a formal ritualized family meal. There are roles in the Seder night for young and old.

Jewish law, as pertaining to the Passover sacrifice, mandated that the roasted sacrifice be consumed in groups and that the groups should be organized prior to the holiday. Families were together the fateful night of the first Passover Seder as the Egyptian first-borns were slain outside their homes and left Egypt together as families, part of a larger community having suffered collectively.

The Haggadah that has been used for over a thousand years is clearly formulated to incorporate our immediate family young and old, and our circle of friends and guests. Its texts includes directives from the hosts to outsiders, directives from parent to child, and customs directed specifically at the youngest among us. As such, the Seder ceremony embraces family and community as much as it is a call for Jewish continuity.

Introduction to the Theme of Gratitude

It is telling that most of the commentary found in the popular Haggadot focus on only a third of the text in the Haggadah. Two-thirds of the Seder ceremony is read or sung without much analysis or fanfare. What comprises this under-analyzed portion? It is the Hallel or liturgy of praise. Praise to God for having rescued the Jewish nation from Egypt, for having given the Jewish nation their identity and mission with the Torah revelation at Mount Sinai, and for having brought them to the footstep of their homeland Israel. The theme of these portions of the Haggadah is that of gratitude and it is found throughout the Haggadah.

The theme of gratitude – for what we have received in the past and for what we may have now – as inspired by the Haggadah is the theme of this evening. It is an important message for all of us and for our children.

בְּשַׁבָּת מַתְחִילִין

לשבת: וַיְהִי עֶרֶב וַיְהִי בֹקֶר יוֹם הַשִּׁשִּׁי. וַיְכֻלּוּ הַשָּׁמַיִם וְהָאָרֶץ וְכָל צְבָאָם. וַיְכַל אֱלֹהִים בַּיּוֹם הַשְּׁבִיעִי מְלַאכְתּוֹ אֲשֶׁר עָשָׂה וַיִּשְׁבֹּת בַּיּוֹם הַשְּׁבִיעִי מִכָּל מְלַאכְתּוֹ אֲשֶׁר עָשָׂה. וַיְבָרֶךְ אֱלֹהִים אֶת יוֹם הַשְּׁבִיעִי וַיְקַדֵּשׁ אוֹתוֹ כִּי בוֹ שָׁבַת מִכָּל מְלַאכְתּוֹ אֲשֶׁר בָּרָא אֱלֹהִים לַעֲשׂוֹת.

סַבְרִי מָרָנָן וְרַבָּנָן וְרַבּוֹתַי

בָּרוּךְ אַתָּה יְיָ אֱלֹהֵינוּ מֶלֶךְ הָעוֹלָם בּוֹרֵא פְּרִי הַגָּפֶן.

בָּרוּךְ אַתָּה יְיָ אֱלֹהֵינוּ מֶלֶךְ הָעוֹלָם, אֲשֶׁר בָּחַר בָּנוּ מִכָּל עָם וְרוֹמְמָנוּ מִכָּל לָשׁוֹן וְקִדְּשָׁנוּ בְּמִצְוֹתָיו. וַתִּתֶּן לָנוּ יְיָ אֱלֹהֵינוּ בְּאַהֲבָה (בשבת: שַׁבָּתוֹת לִמְנוּחָה וּ) מוֹעֲדִים לְשִׂמְחָה, חַגִּים וּזְמַנִּים לְשָׂשׂוֹן, אֶת יוֹם (הַשַּׁבָּת הַזֶּה וְאֶת יוֹם) חַג הַמַּצּוֹת הַזֶּה, זְמַן חֵרוּתֵנוּ (בְּאַהֲבָה), מִקְרָא קֹדֶשׁ, זֵכֶר לִיצִיאַת מִצְרָיִם. כִּי בָנוּ בָחַרְתָּ וְאוֹתָנוּ קִדַּשְׁתָּ מִכָּל הָעַמִּים, (וְשַׁבָּת) וּמוֹעֲדֵי קָדְשֶׁךָ (בְּאַהֲבָה וּבְרָצוֹן,) בְּשִׂמְחָה וּבְשָׂשׂוֹן הִנְחַלְתָּנוּ. **בָּרוּךְ אַתָּה יְיָ, מְקַדֵּשׁ (הַשַׁבָּת וְ)יִשְׂרָאֵל וְהַזְּמַנִּים.**

כשחל ליל הסדר במוצאי שבת מוסיפים כאן ברכות הבדלה:

בָּרוּךְ אַתָּה יְיָ אֱלֹהֵינוּ מֶלֶךְ הָעוֹלָם, בּוֹרֵא מְאוֹרֵי הָאֵשׁ. בָּרוּךְ אַתָּה יְיָ אֱלֹהֵינוּ מֶלֶךְ הָעוֹלָם הַמַּבְדִּיל בֵּין קֹדֶשׁ לְחֹל, בֵּין אוֹר לְחֹשֶׁךְ, בֵּין יִשְׂרָאֵל לָעַמִּים, בֵּין יוֹם הַשְּׁבִיעִי לְשֵׁשֶׁת יְמֵי הַמַּעֲשֶׂה. בֵּין קְדֻשַּׁת שַׁבָּת לִקְדֻשַּׁת יוֹם טוֹב הִבְדַּלְתָּ, וְאֶת יוֹם הַשְּׁבִיעִי מִשֵּׁשֶׁת יְמֵי הַמַּעֲשֶׂה קִדַּשְׁתָּ. הִבְדַּלְתָּ וְקִדַּשְׁתָּ אֶת עַמְּךָ יִשְׂרָאֵל בִּקְדֻשָּׁתֶךָ. בָּרוּךְ אַתָּה יְיָ הַמַּבְדִּיל בֵּין קֹדֶשׁ לְקֹדֶשׁ.

בָּרוּךְ אַתָּה יְיָ אֱלֹהֵינוּ מֶלֶךְ הָעוֹלָם, שֶׁהֶחֱיָנוּ וְקִיְּמָנוּ וְהִגִּיעָנוּ לַזְּמַן הַזֶּה.

שׁוֹתֶה רֹב כּוֹס הַיַּיִן בַּהֲסִיבָּה שְׂמֹאל.

When the festival occurs on Shabbat

The sixth day. And the heavens and the earth and all their hosts were completed. And on the seventh day God finished His work which He had made, and He rested on the seventh day from all His work which He had made. And God blessed the seventh day and made it holy, for on it He rested from all His work which God created to make.

Blessed are You, Hashem, our God, King of the universe, who creates the fruit of the vine. Blessed are You, God, our God, King of the universe, who has chosen us from among all people, and raised us above all tongues, and made us holy through His commandments. And You, God, our God, have given us in love (On Shabbat add: Shabbat for rest and) festivals for happiness, feasts and festive seasons for rejoicing (this Shabbat-day and) the day of this Feast of Matzot and this Festival of holy convocation, the Season of our Freedom (in love), a holy convocation, commemorating the departure from Egypt. For You have chosen us and sanctified us from all the nations, and You have given us as a heritage Your holy (Shabbat and) Festivals (in love and favor), in happiness and joy. Blessed are You, God, who sanctifies (the Shabbat and) Israel and the festive seasons. **Blessed are You, Hashem, our God, King of the universe, who has granted us life, sustained us, and enabled us to reach this occasion.**

When the festival falls on Saturday night add the following blessing of Havdala:
Blessed are You, God, our God, King of the universe, who creates the lights of fire. Blessed are You, God, our God, King of the universe, who makes a distinction between sacred and profane, between light and darkness, between Israel and the nations, between the seventh day and the six work-days. You have made a distinction between the holiness of the Shabbat and the holiness of the festival, and You have sanctified the seventh day above the six work-days. You have set apart and made holy Your people Israel with Your holiness. **Blessed are You, Hashem, who makes a distinction between holy and holy.**

Drink the majority of the cup of wine while seated, reclining on the left side

Holiday of Freedom

Pesach, too, is a holiday which we celebrate our hopes for the future. It is a holiday which proclaims that man should and has to be free. It celebrates the fact that only if we are optimistic about the future, if we believe that God will help us overcome all inhumanity, can we truly celebrate Pesach. If a person no longer believes that the Jewish people have a covenant with God, if they negate circumcision or worship idols, then they really have no place at the seder. Pesach is a holiday in which we assert that there is hope and we strengthen each other in our hopes. Pesach is a holiday of commitment. Jews who cannot be committed to the holiday of freedom do not belong. All those who convert to Judaism or those who are almost Jews can participate. On Pesach, we declare that God can help us and God will Help us.

Rabbi Joseph Radinsky

Redemption is Transformation

A major theme of Pesach is transformation. In a physical sense, the Jews were transformed from slaves to free people. Additionally, there is the religious transformation mentioned twice: the first "in the beginning our fathers served idols" and the second is from a fledging Jewish nation without an articulated "mission statement" to a people with a written "constitution" – the Torah.

The transformations can be understood both on the individual level and on the communal level.

Every Jewish holiday has a general theme or objective. Every holiday is designed to be transformative in its own way. On Yom Kippur the objective is to personally reflect on what went wrong and how we might do better. On Chanukah the objective to remember the historical military victory and providential guidance of the past to influence us today. On Shavuot the goal is to reflect on the nature of the revelation of the Torah and to reaccept its principals and requirements. Every Jewish holiday is designed to change us, to recharge us, and motivate us to improve our relationships with our fellow man, how we feel about ourselves, and with God.

The Warsaw Ghetto Uprising

The Jews of the Warsaw ghetto began their revolt against the Nazis on the first night of Pesach.

Pesach has come to the ghetto again.
The lore-laden words of the Seder are said,
And the cup of the prophet Elijah awaits,
But the Angel of Death has intruded, instead.
As always – the German snarls his commands.
As always – the words sharpened- up and precise.
As always – the fate of more Jews in his hands:
Who shall love, who shall die, this Passover night.
But no more will the Jews to the slaughter be led.
The truculent jibes of the Nazis are past.
And the lintels and doorposts tonight will be red
With the blood of free Jews who will fight to the last.

Binem Heller

Some questions regarding change – transformation – to contemplate:

Does change to an individual or nation come quickly or slowly and progressively?

Can the initial moment of change be pinpointed?

What are the obstacles to change?

וּרְחַץ

נוֹטְלִים אֶת הַיָדַיִם וְאֵין מְבָרְכִים "עַל נְטִילַת יָדַיִם".

כַּרְפַּס

טוֹבְלִין כַּרְפַּס פָּחוֹת מִכְּזַיִת בְּמֵי מֶלַח, וּמְבָרְכִין. וִיכַוֵּן בְּבִרְכָתוֹ גַּם אֶת הַמָּרוֹר:

בָּרוּךְ אַתָּה יְיָ אֱלֹהֵינוּ מֶלֶךְ הָעוֹלָם, בּוֹרֵא פְּרִי הָאֲדָמָה.

What If Tomorrow There Is No Bread?

Every year, on Seder night, when I break the matzah in half and hide the afikoman, I am overcome with emotion as I recall my first day in Israel.

I arrived in Kibbutz Kedma together with other children, all of us new immigrants who had arrived in Israel without our parents after World War II. We were hungry, penniless and exhausted from our wandering and constant hunger.

On the table in the dining room, there were all kinds of delicious foods. There were plenty of vegetables, cheeses and bread, and we could take as much as we wanted. I couldn't believe that at the next meal, we would also have as much bread to eat as we wanted.

Urchatz

Wash hands without reciting the blessing.

Karpas

Take less than a kezayit (the volume of one olive) of the karpas, dip it into salt-water or vinegar, and recite the following blessing.

When reciting this blessing have in mind that it is also for the bitter herbs of the maror

Blessed are You, Hashem, our God, King of the universe, who creates the fruit of the earth

---

> There were many days in Europe when I could think of nothing else except bread – of which there was never enough. There were many nights when I went to bed hungry. I would remain awake for hours, with my stomach growling from hunger, dreaming of bread. But now in Israel there was so much food.
>
> What did I do in those first days in the kibbutz when we sat down at the table, loaded down with so many foods I was filled with fear that maybe there wouldn't be any bread the next day. So I would break each slice of bread I received in half; I would eat half, and the other half I would hide in my pocket. I could not forget the days in which I was never sure if there would be bread tomorrow.
>
> **Bina Talitman**

יַחַץ

עוֹרֵךְ הַסֵּדֶר לוֹקֵחַ אֶת הַמַּצָּה הָאֶמְצָעִית וְחוֹצֶה אוֹתָהּ לִשְׁנֵי חֲלָקִים בִּלְתִּי שָׁוִוים. אֶת הַחֵלֶק הַקָּטָן מַשְׁאִירִים בֵּין הַשְּׁתַּיִים הַשְּׁלֵמוֹת, וְאִילּוּ אֶת הַחֵלֶק הַגָּדוֹל מַטְמִינִים לַאֲפִיקוֹמָן.

Passover of 1945

There is no limit to human troubles and pain. I have already survived the concentration camp at Buchenwald, that hell, where that terrible specter of death – the crematorium – burns day and night. Now I find myself in another concentration camp, Dora.

I work in a deep tunnel beneath high mountains that proudly rise thousands of meters into the sky. Who is interested in the magic of nature, which for us is a disappointment and a curse? The sun shines, but it doesn't reach us. We are deep in the tunnel, like living in their graves. Our tortured and shrunken bodies freeze in the cold; the constant hunger and hard work lead us toward a slow death. Every day tortured comrades fall, and their bodies are burned in the crematorium.

Once again I lie on a straw-filled paper sack on a bunk during the Seder night of 1945, enveloped in a world of dreams, fantasies, and associations. My neighbor, a fellow Tshenstokhover by the name of Shimen Gostinsky, looks at me with pleading eyes and asks me a concentration camp question for Passover:

"Tell me, will this hell last much longer? I beg you, say at least a few comforting words. I can't stand this any longer."

Yisroel-Yoysef Kutner, the cantor, the deeply religious Jew who has survived all these troubles together with me and withstood various religious temptations without allowing his spirit to be broken for a minute, comes to my bunk. But this time, he is unable to break off even a small bit

 Rachatz

Take the middle matzah and break it into two, one piece larger than the other.
The larger piece is set aside to serve as afikoman.
The smaller piece is put back, between the two matzot.

---

of matzah for me, as he did the previous year.

He hungers, like everyone else, and has just the meager bit of risen bread that he receives in the concentration camp. He brings me a different gift, in the form of comfort and hope, saying to me: "Don't lose hope. It is expressly written that one is a slave for six years and in the seventh year one is set free. We have been under Hitler's tyranny and enslavement for six Passovers now. Soon we will be redeemed, and next Passover we will celebrate properly the season of four redemption.

Tragic and bitter days came, accompanied by hunger, pain, loneliness, blows, heavy labor, mass deaths, and evacuation.

In our new location in the concentration camp at Bergen-Belsen, Yisroel Yoysef's prophecy came true; the liberation came on the fifteenth of April, 1945. It brought with it glorious, exalted moments of pure joy, new hopes, encouragement, and strengthened will.

The appearance of the first English tanks, the joyful sound of the radio speakers announcing the Allied victory, and the friendliness of the victorious soldiers' fall seemed a kingdom of dreams and fantasies.

With the fall of Nazis, Passover is indeed the festival of liberation for me. Through a miracle, I have been rescued from Nazi bondage. Yet I feel like a solitary twig from a ruined garden.

Binyomin Orenshtayn

מַגִּיד

עוֹרֵךְ הַסֵּדֶר מְגַלֶּה אֶת הַמַּצּוֹת מַגְבִּיהַּ אֶת הַקְּעָרָה וְאוֹמֵר בְּקוֹל רָם:

הָא לַחְמָא עַנְיָא

דִּי אֲכָלוּ אַבְהָתָנָא בְּאַרְעָא דְמִצְרָיִם.
כָּל דִּכְפִין יֵיתֵי וְיֵכוֹל, כָּל דִּצְרִיךְ יֵיתֵי וְיִפְסַח.
הָשַׁתָּא הָכָא, לְשָׁנָה הַבָּאָה בְּאַרְעָא דְיִשְׂרָאֵל.
הָשַׁתָּא עַבְדֵי, לְשָׁנָה הַבָּאָה בְּנֵי חוֹרִין.

The Road Taken

One of the seniors that year began with what seasoned graduation-goers immediately recognized, and dreaded, as a numbing cliche: a reference to Robert Frost's "The Road Not Taken."

Now there's nothing wrong with individuality, to be sure. But all the same, the poem and its purported point are rather heavily traveled themselves, having become staples of countless literature classes, poetry recitals — and graduations.

The poem's narrator, she explained, seems to take pride in having chosen from the "two roads diverged in a yellow wood" the one "less traveled by" — a choice that, looked back upon "somewhere ages and ages hence," would turn out to have "made all the difference."

The graduation speaker, though, begged to take issue with the idea that the less traveled path is necessarily the more valiant choice. The life-path, for example, that she and her classmates had come to value most was a road well-worn indeed, trodden by countless Jewish generations that came this way before our own arrival here.

We hold our heads high, she declared, as we endeavor to walk in their very footsteps, filled with pride at the chance to follow such inspiring predecessors, and to wear as did they, the hallowed mantle of Torah and

The leader of the Seder uncovers the matzot,
raises the Seder Plate with the matzot and says aloud:

This is the bread of affliction

that our fathers ate in the land of Egypt. Whoever is hungry, let him come and eat; whoever is in need, let him come and conduct the Seder of Passover. This year [we are] here; next year in the land of Israel. This year [we are] slaves; next year [we will be] free people.

. . . .

Jewish observance. Judaism, after all, she explained, is not about blazing new paths but about cherishing and preserving time-honored ones.

It was, ironically, a rebellious message in its own way. It boldly shunned the conformity-in-the-guise-of-individualism proffered at every turn by our open, freedom-loving society, a society that trumpets self-celebration, self-fulfillment, self respect, self.

What this seventeen-year-old was saying was that our undeniable value as individuals must be tempered by, even made subservient to, our value as links over history in a chain of life and family and peoplehood - as members of an eternal community of belief and commitment.

It is a message, truly, for our times. In an age of emotional alienation, marital discord, rampant consumerism and instant gratification, nothing could be healthier to digest than the fact that we have not only desires but responsibilities, that we were gifted with our lives to fulfill something more than ourselves.

Those who come to recognize that fact, and its upshot, will likely one day, ages hence, look back and realize that, indeed, it really made all the difference.

Rabbi Avi Shafran

Israel As The Center Of The World

Civilization, as we know it, depends on the survival and well-being of the state of Israel. It is a nexus which many, if not most, would deny; this mistake is one of the central tragedies of our age, for we may learn too late that the welfare of the Jewish homeland is a litmus test for the welfare of freedom and justice wherever they may be.

The effort to demonize and destroy the Jewish state — the embodiment of the self-determination of the Jewish people — is the face of modern anti-Semitism.

The corrosive effect of this anti-Semitism and anti-Zionism on the central tenets of international law and order is clearest at the United Nations — the organization founded on the ashes of the Jewish people.

The U.N. Charter declares the equality of all nations large and small; the Universal Declaration of Human Rights, also celebrating its 60th anniversary this year, insists upon the equality of all races and religions. And yet, responsibility for the globalization of anti-Semitism lies with the U.N. itself. Through the U.N., the enemies of Israel have corrupted the system of the international protection of human rights, the principles of combating racism and xenophobia, and the elementary laws of self-defense.

Let us hope that we recognize in time that those who aim first to justify Israel's annihilation, aim second at the remainder of the free world.

Anne Bayefsky

The Pesach Sacrifice: Its Positive and Negative Commandments

Every sacrifice that was offered in the Beis HaMikdash had its specific purpose and its distinctive halachos. The Rambam enumerated no fewer than eleven Scriptural commandments governing the korban Pesach, the Passover sacrifice – a number not reached by any other korban.

One of these commandments is indicated by an interesting translation in Onkelos' Aramaic rendition of the Torah known as the Targum. The Torah says (which is usually translated): No alien shall eat thereof" (Exodus 12:43). Not so the Targum, which translates: "Any Jew who becomes an apostate (Meshumad) shall not eat thereof." The author of *Meshech Chochmah* explains that the very wording of the commandment indicated this meaning. To whom, he asks, is the Torah speaking? To a Jew? Then it should say, "You shall not feed the korban Pesach to any alien." To a non-Jew? He is not obligated to observe most of the Torah. We must therefore say that this verse forbids an apostate Jew to partake of the korban Pesach.

An original point is made in this connection by the author of Pardess Yosef. Why is it that on Yom Kippur eve we open the Kol Nidrei service with a solemn declaration allowing transgressors of this sort to join us in our fasting and prayers, yet on Pesach night we strictly insist that they keep away? And he answers his own question. When a Jew, however far away he has wandered, wishes to join us in our prayers and fasts, we may reasonably assume that we discern a spark of serious goodwill, which we are anxious to encourage. If, however, that spark awakens when the aroma of the festive roast reaches his nostrils, and all he wants is to join us in our feasts and joys, we say, "Such partners we can do without."

Rabbi S.Y. Zevin

Bread as a Symbol of Transformation

Matza: Whether you refer to it as the poor man's bread – the bread of affliction – or the food that was baked in a hurry to leave Egypt, it is still bread. Bread, due to its simple components, its universal use in its numerous varieties since the beginning of civilization, and our dependence on its central role in our diet, has become a metaphor for life itself. The image of bread has, at times, come to symbolize money, sustenance, and worldly pursuits. How fascinating that bread, in this case, matza, was chosen as a core symbol for Pesach because matza is a transformational food.

In a lecture on bread production, Peter Reinhart describes bread as a transitional food. He describes that bread begins as wheat, which is, of course, a living plant. It is then harvested, killed in the process, and the wheat kernels are collected. First transformation. The wheat germs are ground and mixed with water, still a non-living substance until yeast is added; now the dough is a living substance. Second transformation. The dough is kneaded and baked whereupon this living mass is transformed by heat and killed in the process. Third transformation. Finally the bread is consumed by humans enhancing life. Fourth transformation.

In matza, this transformation process is interrupted. This interruption should give us pause to reflect on our own transformation as Jews, as individuals, as families, and as communities. As this interruption is temporary, we will hopefully resume eating regular bread in the near future, but with the realization that our personal transformation should be one of purpose and fulfillment.

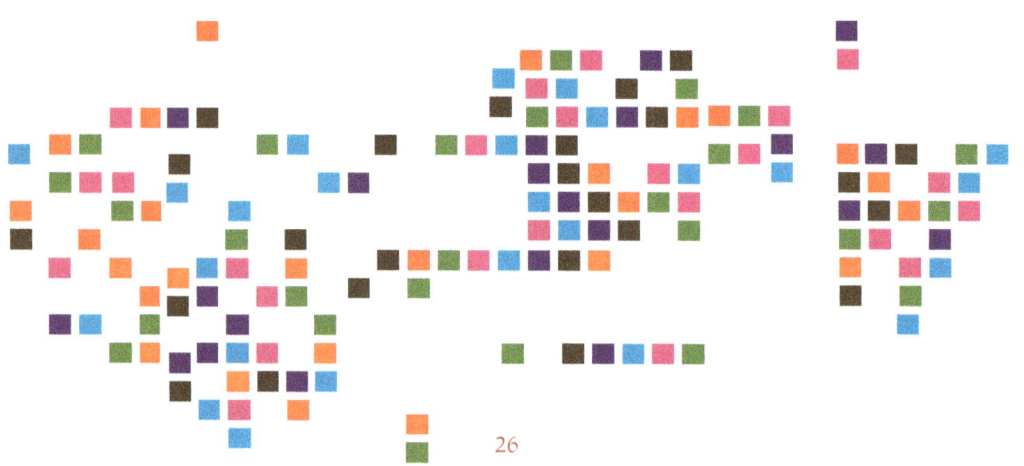

Beginnings of Acknowledgment

Few of us realize what place this principle of Hakarat Hatov, of acknowledging every favor and kindness, holds at the very foundation of our faith. In the Midrash we read: The Holy, Blessed One declared to the Israelites (as He began the Ten Commandments), I am the Lord your God; but why did He add, who brought you forth out of Egypt (Exodus 20:2). He said to them, in effect, "Beware, take care that you do not turn ungrateful, for ingrates cannot accept the kingship of Heaven" (Mishnat R. Eliezer, 137-389).

Had He begun the Ten Commandments as "the Lord your God who created heaven and earth," there could be ways of throwing off the Divine obligation of the Torah. A person might retort that if He is the Creator, all mankind owes Him allegiance equally; why "pick" on the Jews?

Instead, the Ten Commandments begin with a ringing, imperishable reminder that He rescued our ancestors from a servitude that could have left them a slave people forever. He did this with miracles and wonders, so that no Hebrew there could possibly doubt His existence or His participation. This became a tradition of faith among our people, handed down from one generation to the next, from the exodus itself to this day.

Rabbi Irving M Bunim

The Jewish Mayflower

Three hundred years ago a ship called the Mayflower set sail to the New World. This was a great event in the history of England. Yet I wonder if there is one Englishman who knows at what time the ship set sail? Do the English know how many people embarked on this voyage? What quality of bread did they eat?

Yet more than 3,300 years ago, before the Mayflower set sail, the Jews left Egypt. Every Jew in the world, even in America or Soviet Russia knows on exactly what date they left – the fifteenth of the month of Nisan; everyone knows what kind of bread the Jews ate – Matza. Even today the Jews worldwide eat Matza on the 15th of Nisan. They retell the story of the Exodus and all the troubles Jews have endured since being exiled saying:

"This year, slaves. Next year free!
This year here. Next year in Jerusalem, in Zion, in Eretz Yisrael!"
That is the nature of the Jews.

David Ben Gurion, in a speech to the United Nations, 1947

מֵסִיר הַקְּעָרָה מֵעַל הַשֻּׁלְחָן, מוֹזְגִים לְכָל אֶחָד מֵהַמְסֻבִּים כּוֹס שֵׁנִי.
כַּאן הַבֵּן שׁוֹאֵל אֶת אַרְבַּע הַקֻּשְׁיוֹת.

מַה נִּשְׁתַּנָּה?

מַה נִּשְׁתַּנָּה הַלַּיְלָה הַזֶּה מִכָּל הַלֵּילוֹת

שֶׁבְּכָל הַלֵּילוֹת אָנוּ אוֹכְלִין חָמֵץ וּמַצָּה,
הַלַּיְלָה הַזֶּה כֻּלּוֹ מַצָּה.

שֶׁבְּכָל הַלֵּילוֹת אָנוּ אוֹכְלִין שְׁאָר יְרָקוֹת,
הַלַּיְלָה הַזֶּה מָרוֹר!

שֶׁבְּכָל הַלֵּילוֹת אֵין אָנוּ מַטְבִּילִין אֲפִילוּ פַּעַם אֶחָת,
הַלַּיְלָה הַזֶּה שְׁתֵּי פְעָמִים!

שֶׁבְּכָל הַלֵּילוֹת אָנוּ אוֹכְלִין בֵּין יוֹשְׁבִין וּבֵין מְסֻבִּין,
הַלַּיְלָה הַזֶּה כֻּלָּנוּ מְסֻבִּין!

• •

Beginnings Are Difficult

While not too many of us likely remember what it was like to take our first steps, one can imagine it could be quite a daunting task. An action as simple as walking, which we take completely for granted, probably seems to the untrained toddler an unreachable goal. Yet we urge our young ones on. We know the secret: Once they get the hang of it (and fall down a few hundred times), they'll be prancing around the house and discovering things and places they weren't able to reach before they

The tray with the matzot is moved aside, and the second cup is poured for everyone.
Now the child asks "Mah Nishtana?".

Mah Nishtana?

What makes this night different from all [other] nights? On all nights we eat chametz or matzah, **On this night only matzah.**

On all nights we eat any kind of vegetables, **On this night maror!**

On all nights we need not dip even once, **On this night we do so twice!**

On all nights we eat sitting upright or reclining, **On this night we all recline!**

. . . .

learned. Once they learn to walk, it will become second nature. They will move on to greater challenges and new experiences.

As we grow, we accumulate skills, talents, and abilities that help us to interact with others and with the world. The learning/growth experience is almost always the same. During the initial stages, it takes no less than a leap of faith to believe that one day we'll achieve mastery in what now seems so unreachable. The more times we traverse the learning curve, the more confidence we attain that if we persevere, it can be done.

Perhaps we have failed to understand that the same learning/growth process – encompassing all stages from disbelief to mastery – applies not only to physical growth and tangible skills, but also to spiritual growth and devotion. We read in this week's parsha (19:5-6): "And now, if you will listen to My voice... you shall be to Me the most beloved treasure of all peoples... and you shall be to Me a holy nation." What does Hashem mean when He asks us to listen to Him "now?" Does this imply that later we can ignore Him? Rashi explains: "If you listen to Me now – and accept the Torah upon yourselves, it will become sweet and pleasant for you in due time, for all beginnings are difficult."

Just like once the child learns to walk, there's no looking back, so too, once a person has truly traversed a growth area …, it becomes second nature. He's now ready to conquer new vistas…. The problem is we so seldom get past the stage of taking "baby steps." We're forever bogged down with getting over the initial stages of growth, and waste our entire lives without ever realizing that with just a little more effort and conviction, we could have grown and achieved mastery in so many areas (both physical and spiritual).

True, growth does involve a few scrapes and bruises along the way, but if we persevere, they will one day become a distant memory.

Rabbi Eliyahu Hoffmann

All Questions Are Permitted

On this evening, all questions are not only permitted, but invited. Still, we begin by examining the traditional four questions which illustrate four possible attitudes toward life: that of the wise son, who knows the question and asks it; that of the wicked son, who knows the question but refuses to ask it; that of the simple son, who knows the question but is indifferent to it; and finally, that of the ignorant son, who does not know the question and therefore is unable to ask.

And then, there is my own anguish. What can we do so as not to forget the question? What can we do to defeat oblivion? What significance does Passover have, if not to keep our memories alive? To be Jewish is to assume the burden of the past, to include it in our concerns for the present and for the future.

Elie Wiesel

Pesach Rules

Hashem said to Moses and Aaron, "This is the decree of the Pesach-offering: no alienated person may eat from it. Every slave of a man, who was bought for money, you shall circumcise him; then he may eat of it. A sojourner and a hired laborer may not eat it. In one house shall it be eaten; you shall not remove any of the meat from the house to the outside, and you shall not break a bone in it. The entire assembly of Israel shall perform it."

Exodus 43-47

...Also we know that in ancient days, you just could not invite anybody to come to your seder whom you met at shul that night. You had to be part of a group who had gotten together and designated a particular pascal lamb to be sacrificed. The pascal lamb was sacrificed from noon until dusk. You had to be part of that group before noon. We also know that you could not go from one seder to another in ancient days.

Rabbi Joseph Radinsky

מֵנִיחַ אֶת הַקְּעָרָה עַל הַשֻּׁלְחָן.
הַמַּצוֹת תִּהְיֶינָה מְגֻלּוֹת בִּשְׁעַת אֲמִירַת הַהַגָּדָה.

עֲבָדִים הָיִינוּ

לְפַרְעֹה בְּמִצְרָיִם (דברים ו' כ"א),
וַיּוֹצִיאֵנוּ יְיָ אֱלֹהֵינוּ מִשָּׁם בְּיָד חֲזָקָה וּבִזְרֹעַ נְטוּיָה.
וְאִלּוּ לֹא הוֹצִיא הַקָּדוֹשׁ בָּרוּךְ הוּא
אֶת אֲבוֹתֵינוּ מִמִּצְרַיִם, הֲרֵי אָנוּ וּבָנֵינוּ וּבְנֵי בָנֵינוּ
מְשֻׁעְבָּדִים הָיִינוּ לְפַרְעֹה בְּמִצְרָיִם.
וַאֲפִילוּ כֻּלָּנוּ חֲכָמִים, כֻּלָּנוּ נְבוֹנִים, כֻּלָּנוּ זְקֵנִים,
כֻּלָּנוּ יוֹדְעִים אֶת הַתּוֹרָה,
מִצְוָה עָלֵינוּ לְסַפֵּר בִּיצִיאַת מִצְרָיִם.
וְכָל הַמַּרְבֶּה לְסַפֵּר בִּיצִיאַת מִצְרַיִם הֲרֵי זֶה מְשֻׁבָּח.

Gratitude

This past Shabbos my family held a mass confab in honor of my grandmother, who is celebrating, thank God, her 90th birthday.

In my dvar torah at this get-together, I focused on one of the lessons my grandmother has modeled for me: Eternal gratitude. My grandmother escaped the camps in Europe and came to America, raised three daughters with her husband, lost her husband thirty-plus years ago, has dealt with all sorts of challenges, and throughout all of it, she has thanked God for all that she has.

I was reminded of the Shirah, which we read in shul on Shabbos, the Jews' song of praise to God, with which they celebrated their passage through the Sea and the final destruction of their Egyptian slave drivers. But I was also reminded of the lack of song after so many other Divine favors – after

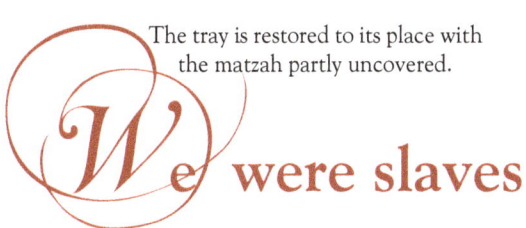

The tray is restored to its place with the matzah partly uncovered.

We were slaves to Pharaoh in Egypt, (Deuteronomy 6:21) and Hashem, our God, took us out from there with a strong hand and with an outstretched arm. If the Holy One, blessed be He, had not taken our fathers out of Egypt, then we, our children and our children's children would have remained enslaved to Pharaoh in Egypt. Even if all of us were wise, all of us understanding, all of us knowing the Torah, we would still be obligated to discuss the exodus from Egypt; and everyone who discusses the exodus from Egypt at length is praiseworthy.

- -

The Rambam on Freedom

Free will is granted to all men. If one desires to turn himself to the path of good and be righteous, the choice is his. Should he desire to turn to the path of evil and be wicked, the choice is his.

Each person is fit to be righteous like Moses, our teacher, or wicked, like Jeroboam. (Similarly,) he may be wise or foolish, merciful or cruel, miserly or generous, or (acquire) any other character traits. There is no one who compels him, sentences him, or leads him towards either of these two paths. Rather, he, on his own initiative and decision, tends to the path he chooses.

Were God to decree that an individual would be righteous or wicked or that there would be a quality which draws a person by his essential nature to any particular path (of behavior), way of thinking, attributes, or

the plagues, after escaping Egypt, after the bitter water was made sweet, after the Manna fell from the heavens, after water came from the stone, etc.

It seems to me that the nation thanked HaShem only for final victory, and not for partial victories. When they were nervous about tomorrow's bread and water, they didn't thank for today's. When the Egyptians yet lived, they didn't thank for today's freedom. There was no trust. It was only after a complete victory that they were able to feel comfortable and safe, and express gratitude.

This is natural, of course. Sincere thanking is difficult, as an expression of both humility and trust. But my grandmother has always expressed thanks, for whatever she has received – and this is a lesson we see in many elements of Judaism.

Rabbi Mordechai Torczyner

deeds – how could He command us through (the words of) the prophets: "Do this," "Do not do this," "Improve your behavior," or "Do not follow after your wickedness?"

What place would there be for the entire Torah?

He desired that man have free choice and be responsible for his deeds, without being pulled or forced. Rather, he, on his own initiative, with the knowledge which God has granted him, will do anything that man is able to do.

Therefore, he is judged according to his deeds.

One might ask: Since The Holy One, blessed be He, knows everything that will occur before it comes to pass, does He or does He not know whether a person will be righteous or wicked?

If He knows that he will be righteous, (it appears) impossible for him not to be righteous. However, if one would say that despite His knowledge that he would be righteous, it is possible for him to be wicked, then His knowledge would be incomplete.

Human knowledge cannot comprehend this concept in its entirety for just as it is beyond the potential of man to comprehend and conceive the essential nature of the Creator, as (Exodus 33:20) states: "No man will perceive, Me and live," so, too, it is beyond man's potential to comprehend and conceive the Creator's knowledge

Rabbi Moses Maimonides

מַעֲשֶׂה

בְּרַבִּי אֱלִיעֶזֶר וְרַבִּי יְהוֹשֻׁעַ
וְרַבִּי אֶלְעָזָר בֶּן עֲזַרְיָה וְרַבִּי עֲקִיבָא וְרַבִּי טַרְפוֹן
שֶׁהָיוּ מְסֻבִּין בִּבְנֵי בְרַק,
וְהָיוּ מְסַפְּרִים בִּיצִיאַת מִצְרַיִם
כָּל אוֹתוֹ הַלַּיְלָה
עַד שֶׁבָּאוּ תַלְמִידֵיהֶם וְאָמְרוּ לָהֶם:
רַבּוֹתֵינוּ, הִגִּיעַ זְמַן קְרִיאַת שְׁמַע שֶׁל שַׁחֲרִית.

"The Wolves Within"

An old Grandfather, whose grandson came to him with anger at a schoolmate who had done him an injustice, said, "Let me tell you a story. I too, at times, have felt a great hate for those that have taken so much, with no sorrow for what they do. But hate wears you down, and does not hurt your enemy. It is like taking poison and wishing your enemy would die. I have struggled with these feelings many times."

He continued, "It is as if there are two wolves inside me; one is good and does no harm. He lives in harmony with all around him and does not take offense when no offense was intended. He will only fight when it is right to do so, and in the right way."

It happened

that Rabbi Eliezer, Rabbi Joshua, Rabbi Elazar ben Azaryah, Rabbi Akiva and Rabbi Tarphon were reclining [at a seder] in B'nei Berak. They were discussing the exodus from Egypt all that night, until their students came and told them: "Our Masters! The time has come for reciting the morning Shema!"

"But the other wolf, ah! He is full of anger. The littlest thing will set him into a fit of temper. He fights everyone, all the time, for no reason. He cannot think because his anger and hate are so great. It is hard to live with these two wolves inside me, for both of them try to dominate my spirit."

The boy looked intently into his Grandfather's eye and asked, "Which one wins, Grandfather?"

The Grandfather solemnly said, "The one I feed."

Anonymous

אָמַר רַבִּי אֶלְעָזָר בֶּן עֲזַרְיָה:
הֲרֵי אֲנִי כְּבֶן שִׁבְעִים שָׁנָה,
וְלֹא זָכִיתִי שֶׁתֵּאָמֵר יְצִיאַת מִצְרַיִם בַּלֵּילוֹת
עַד שֶׁדְּרָשָׁהּ בֶּן זוֹמָא:
שֶׁנֶּאֱמַר: "לְמַעַן תִּזְכֹּר אֶת יוֹם צֵאתְךָ
מֵאֶרֶץ מִצְרַיִם כֹּל יְמֵי חַיֶּיךָ". (דברים ט"ז ג')
"יְמֵי חַיֶּיךָ" – הַיָּמִים,
"כֹּל יְמֵי חַיֶּיךָ" – הַלֵּילוֹת.

וַחֲכָמִים אוֹמְרִים:
"יְמֵי חַיֶּיךָ" – הָעוֹלָם הַזֶּה,
"כֹּל יְמֵי חַיֶּיךָ" – לְהָבִיא לִימוֹת הַמָּשִׁיחַ.

A Discourse on Free Will

In his *Discourse on Free Will*, Rabbi Eliyahu Eliezer Dessler describes how the area of free will differs for each and every person, based on education and other factors, and how it shifts constantly. It is only possible to speak of the exercise of free will, he writes, at that point where a person's apprehension of the truth, i.e., what is right, is in perfect equipoise with a countervailing desire. Precisely at that point, nothing besides the person himself determines the outcome.

Rabbi Dessler employs the spatial metaphor of a battlefield to capture the process. The point at which the battle is joined is the point of free will. Behind the battle line is captured territory – the area where a person feels no temptation to do other than what he perceives as right. And behind the enemy lines are all those areas in which a person does not

Rabbi Eleazar

ben Azaryah said: "I am like a man of seventy years old, yet I did not succeed in proving that the exodus from Egypt must be mentioned at night – until Ben Zoma explained it: "It is said, That you may remember the day you left Egypt all the days of your life;' (Deuteronomy 17:3) now 'the days of your life' refers to the days, [and the additional word] 'all' indicates the inclusion of the nights!"

The sages, however, said: "The days of your life' refers to the present-day world; and 'all' indicates the inclusion of the days of Mashiach."

---

yet have the ability to choose.

The battlefront moves constantly. With every victory – every choice to do what is right – a person advances. And he retreats with every defeat. Pharaoh provides the paradigm of the latter. By repeatedly hardening his heart, he finally lost the capacity to exercise his free will.

In a contemporary context, Rabbi Dessler remarked that those who deny the possibility of free will do so because by failing to develop their own will power through the positive exercise of their free will they have lost their freedom.

"You deny free will because you are in fact unfree; you have enslaved yourselves to the evil within you."

Jonathan Rosenblum

Imprisoned in Our Time

The Haggadah stipulates that four cups of wine are to be consumed as part of the Seder. Numerous commentaries describe that the four cups are symbolic of the four types of redemption mentioned in the Torah. The four expressions are: I (God) will take you; I will save them; I will deliver them; and I will take them to be My nation (Exodus 6:6-8). There is a fifth expression of redemption; I will bring you… For this last expression, an allusion to the future, a fifth cup is poured for the prophet Elijah, who, tradition states, will usher a future redemption.

Pesach is a holiday that among other themes highlights redemption. Transformation, which can and should be a goal for everyone, can take on different forms. For some, transformation might be expressed in individual achievement, for example, to participate more at synagogue, to give more charity, to control one's anger, to be a better parent or spouse. Or transformation can occur on a larger scale, such as initiating community reforms and political changes. For other Jews, physical redemption or freedom is an immediate goal.

Gilad Shalit was an Israel Defense Forces soldier held captive in the Hamas-run Gaza Strip from June 2006 until October 2011. Efforts to secure his release as part of a prisoner exchange, via Egyptian mediation, eventually proved unsuccessful.

Twenty-three-year-old Shalit was born in Nahariya to Aviva and Noam, and was raised from the age of two in Mizpe Hila in the Western Galilee. He has an older brother and a younger sister.

When he turned 18, Shalit was drafted into the IDF armored corps. On June 25, 2006, the then 19-year-old corporal and his comrades were manning a post alongside the Israel-Gaza border when Palestinian gunmen opened fire on their position. The gunmen had dug a tunnel underneath the Gaza barrier, allowing them to reach the position undetected. Two IDF soldiers were killed in the attack, three were wounded, and Shalit was led by his captors into Gaza. During his capture, neither the Red Cross nor any other external organization was allowed access to the soldier in order to independently assess his physical and mental condition.

Gilad Shalit thankfully and miraculously returned home to an expectant nation that had collectively held its breath day after day, year after year, unwilling to give up hope for his release from captivity. He was, after five years, finally reunited with his family, community and country along with all who prayed and worked on his behalf. We look forward to the day when those Jews who are still in captivity and still require physical redemption can all truly say: "Today we are *bnei chorin* – today we are all free men."

Excerpted from Haaretz.com

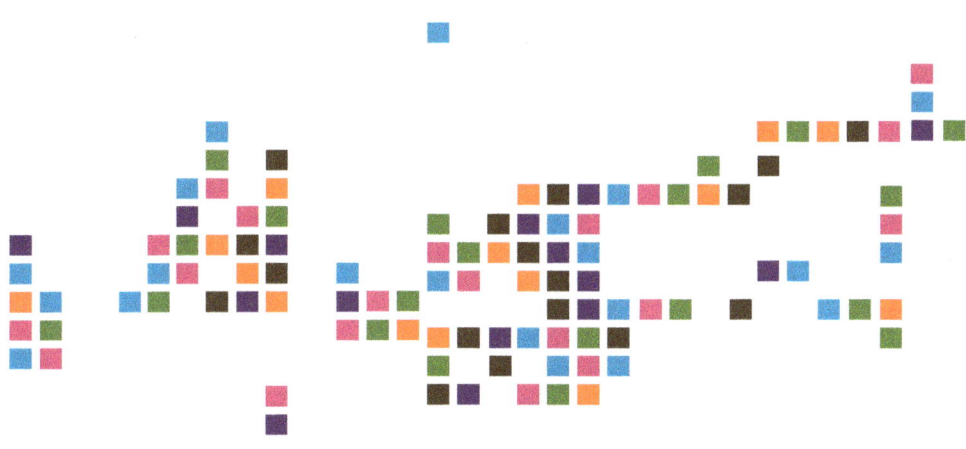

בָּרוּךְ הַמָּקוֹם, בָּרוּךְ הוּא.

בָּרוּךְ שֶׁנָּתַן תּוֹרָה לְעַמּוֹ יִשְׂרָאֵל, בָּרוּךְ הוּא.

כְּנֶגֶד אַרְבָּעָה בָנִים דִּבְּרָה תוֹרָה:
אֶחָד חָכָם,
וְאֶחָד רָשָׁע,
וְאֶחָד תָּם,
וְאֶחָד שֶׁאֵינוֹ יוֹדֵעַ לִשְׁאוֹל.

חָכָם מָה הוּא אוֹמֵר?
"מָה הָעֵדוֹת וְהַחֻקִּים וְהַמִּשְׁפָּטִים אֲשֶׁר צִוָּה יְיָ אֱלֹהֵינוּ אֶתְכֶם?". (דברים ו' כ')
וְאַף אַתָּה אֱמָר־לוֹ כְּהִלְכוֹת הַפֶּסַח:
אֵין מַפְטִירִין אַחַר הַפֶּסַח אֲפִיקוֹמָן.

Power of Community

... AA and OA and all the other "Anonymous" groups have meetings and sponsors because they recognize the power of community. Many people make work-out commitments with a buddy in an effort to stick with it. Peer pressure is a well-documented phenomenon.

While the New England Journal of Medicine piece was focused on eating, particularly obesity, there are even more serious issues at stake. A community that shares our values allows us to grow and thrive. We aspire to live up to the standards it sets. A community with values contrary to our own also has an impact. We are not immune.

Blessed is the Omnipresent One, blessed be He! Blessed is He who gave the Torah to His people Israel, blessed be He!

The Torah speaks of four children:
One is wise, one is wicked,
one is simple
and one does not know how to ask.

The wise one, what does he say? What are the testimonies, the statutes and the laws which Hashem, our God, has commanded you?" (Deuteronomy 6:20) You, in turn, shall instruct him in the laws of Passover, [up to] one is not to eat any dessert after the Passover-lamb.

... if we spend time with people whose focus is spiritual, our focus will be directed in a loftier direction. If we spend time with people who shun malicious slander, we will probably keep our mouths shut. And if we spend time with people whose goal is to actualize their potential and be the best they can be, then we will be motivated to do the same.

Choosing to live in a supportive community makes a big difference to our lives. It's all up to us.

Emuna Braverman

רָשָׁע מָה הוּא אוֹמֵר?
"מָה הָעֲבֹדָה הַזֹּאת לָכֶם?". (שמות י"ב כ"ו)
לָכֶם וְלֹא לוֹ.
וּלְפִי שֶׁהוֹצִיא אֶת עַצְמוֹ מִן הַכְּלָל כָּפַר בְּעִקָּר.
וְאַף אַתָּה הַקְהֵה אֶת שִׁנָּיו, וֶאֱמֹר לוֹ:
"בַּעֲבוּר זֶה עָשָׂה יְיָ לִי
בְּצֵאתִי מִמִּצְרָיִם" (שמות י"ג ח').
לִי וְלֹא לוֹ.
אִילוּ הָיָה שָׁם, לֹא הָיָה נִגְאָל.

To Be Inclusive Not Exclusive

I believe that the most fundamental message of the Passover seder – indeed, of family dynamics, of classroom management and of national policy as well – is to be inclusive and not exclusive, to make everyone feel wanted and accepted rather than merely tolerated or rejected! Indeed, it is in the context of the response to the wicked child that the haggadah teaches that the most basic principle of our faith is to include oneself – as well as everyone who can possibly be included – within the historical community of Israel, to be part of the eternal chain of Jewish being, to be a member of the family! Therefore, the problem with this (the *rasha*/wicked) child's question is not his search for relevance: that is to be applauded and properly responded to. The problem is the fact that he excluded himself from the familial – national celebration; he saw it as applying to "you" and not to "him".

The wicked one, what does he say? "What is this service to you?!" (Exodus 12:26) He says 'to you,' but not to him! By thus excluding himself from the community he has denied that which is fundamental. You, therefore, blunt his teeth and say to him: "It is because of this that Hashem did for me when I left Egypt"; (Exodus 13:8) 'for me' – but not for him! If he had been there, he would not have been redeemed!"

....

Tell him (that is to the rasha/wicked child), says the author of the haggadah, that although we are living thousands of the years after the fact, G-d took me – and him/her as my child – out of Egypt, because we are all one historic family, united by our family celebrations and traditions; tell him that the most important principle of our tradition is to feel oneself an integral part of a family which was once enslaved and is now free – and to re-live this message of the evils of slavery and the glories of freedom because if they happened to our forbears it is as if they happened to us. Since we were formed by them, we are them and they are us! And so is he/she!

Rabbi Shlomo Riskin

תָּם מָה הוּא אוֹמֵר?
"מַה זֹּאת?". (שמות י"ג י"ד)
וְאָמַרְתָּ אֵלָיו:
"בְּחֹזֶק יָד הוֹצִיאָנוּ יְיָ מִמִּצְרַיִם,
מִבֵּית עֲבָדִים". (שמות י"ג י"ד)

וְשֶׁאֵינוֹ יוֹדֵעַ לִשְׁאוֹל,
אַתְּ פְּתַח לוֹ,
שֶׁנֶּאֱמַר: "וְהִגַּדְתָּ לְבִנְךָ בַּיּוֹם הַהוּא לֵאמֹר:
בַּעֲבוּר זֶה עָשָׂה יְיָ לִי בְּצֵאתִי מִמִּצְרָיִם". (שמות י"ג ח')

Concepts in Freedom - Approach #1:
We Are Still Servants to Destructive Pressures of Society

People in the rat race are busy trying to keep up with and surpass the Joneses. They are driven by jealousy, greed and competitiveness. They do not see ultimate meaning in their lives, but want as much fame, fortune and fun as they can get. People in the rat race usually are not evil or corrupt, although some are. Many are simply drawn into the race because they have not thoroughly thought through their philosophy of life or do not have the independence of spirit to stand up for their values and ideals. They are driven by conformism or quasi totalitarianism. They surrender their freedom and autonomy in order to play the game of life according to the rules of the rat race.

The simple one, what does he say?
"What is this?" (Exodus 13:14)
Thus you shall say to him:
"With a strong hand Hashem took us out of Egypt, from the house of slaves." (Exodus 13:14)

As for the one who does not know how to ask, you must initiate him, as it is said:
"You shall tell your child on that day,
'It is because of this that Hashem did for me when I left Egypt.'" (Exodus 13:8)

What are the characteristics of the rat race?

An inordinate emphasis on external matters – good looks, wealth, power, popularity, fame.

A profound feeling that life is a great competition that we must not allow ourselves to fall behind.

An acceptance of standards set by others; a drive toward conformity even at the risk of betraying one's own values; an internalization of standards that compromise our freedom to make responsible choices.

A willingness to abandon ethical standards in order to advance oneself.

Rabbi Marc Angel

"וְהִגַּדְתָּ לְבִנְךָ", יָכוֹל מֵרֹאשׁ חֹדֶשׁ? תַּלְמוּד לוֹמַר: "בַּיּוֹם הַהוּא". אִי בַּיּוֹם הַהוּא, יָכוֹל מִבְּעוֹד יוֹם? תַּלְמוּד לוֹמַר: "בַּעֲבוּר זֶה". "בַּעֲבוּר זֶה" לֹא אָמַרְתִּי, אֶלָּא בְּשָׁעָה שֶׁיֵּשׁ מַצָּה וּמָרוֹר מֻנָּחִים לְפָנֶיךָ.

The Value of Trying

After the exodus from Egypt and not long before the Jews are to enter the land of Israel, Moshe is instructed to establish the cities of refuge where unintentional murderers could flee from the family avenger. Three cities were to be on the east of the Jordon river and three additional cities on the west of the river to be activated only after the entire land of Israel was conquered.

A question can be raised: What is the point of creating the cities east of the Jordon river when they would not even function as cities of refuge, until another three cities in the land of Israel proper would be dedicated for the same purpose? Only after the land was completely captured, would these six cities be activated as cities of refuge. As is well known, Moshe Rabenu was not allowed to enter the land of Israel.

This confronts Moshe with some major issues in his religious commitment. Now that he is not able to fulfill the great mitzvah of living in the land, what is the point in starting a mitzvah, which relates to the actual dwelling in the land but which cannot be completed, since he will never have the opportunity to do so? Nevertheless, Moshe separates these three cities at his earliest opportunity, i.e. when he and the Israelites find themselves at the very site of these cities, in Tran Jordan.

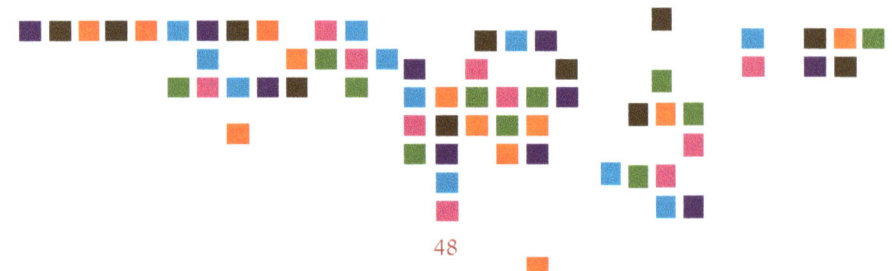

One may think that [the discussion of the exodus] must be from the first of the month. The Torah therefore says, 'On that day.' 'On that day,' however, could mean while it is yet daytime; the Torah therefore says, 'It is because of this.' The expression 'because of this' – can only be said when matzah and maror are placed before you.

• •

> His point is clear and of great meaning: One does not postpone or completely ignore a mitzvah, just because he/she is not sure that he will ever be able to work for, or experience, its completion. On the contrary, one starts to fulfill a mitzvah, whatever the outcome, or the extent of its fulfillment, may be. The reason is clear: Even when one does not complete a mitzvah there is still great value in starting it. Every step in the direction to complete it is a major achievement. And even when, in the end, all that was achieved seems to have been lost, the value of trying to accomplish the mitzvah has a major impact on the human soul. So the holidays often make us wonder why we should try to do teshuva once more when there is a considerable chance that we will not make it all the way this year too. Moshe's example stands out. But despite last year's experience, we clearly do have the possibility to complete the mitzvah of (whatever) this year. And for those who will not succeed, they should not forget that real religious life is not where one finds oneself spiritually, but how hard one tries to get there.
>
> **Yakov Fogelman**

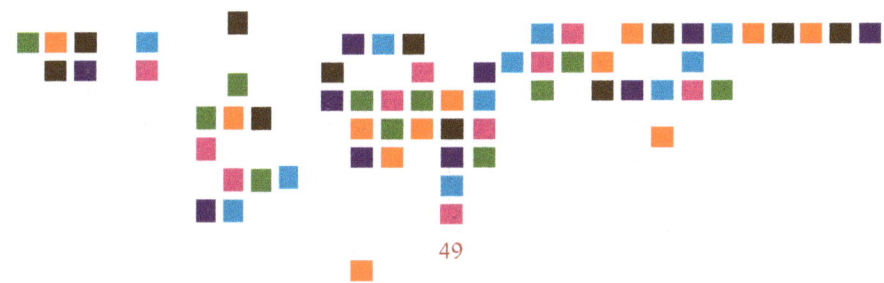

Free At Last

The Haggadah asks us "to imagine that he himself had come out of Egypt." What would have been our thoughts had we personally emerged from Egypt along with the rest of the nascent Jewish nation?

First of all, the former slave is leaving the country ostensibly with his family, indeed his entire community. Friendly faces surround you. But anxiety and fear would naturally surface: Where exactly are we going? What kind of job will I have? Do I get to choose now my schedule, my profession, my leisure activities? Will there be leaders among us? What structure will our community have? The uncertainties of this transition are quieted by the fact that this is a group experience, and the knowledge that we are not alone.

Redemption from slavery, oppression, incarceration, and the underclass occur in our very day, certainly on an individual level. By virtue of hard work, the influence of family and people around them, or by serendipity, individuals redeem themselves from poverty or ignorance to higher levels of education, professional achievement, and socio-economic class.

Consider Cornelius Dupree Jr. who was released from a jail in Dallas, Texas on January 4th 2011. He had served thirty years of a 75-year sentence for a crime that occurred in 1980. Mr. Dupree had maintained his innocence throughout his time in prison, and DNA evidence using modern technology proved that he did not commit the crime for which he spent so long in jail.

Once the DNA was retested, freedom came quickly. "It's a joy to be free again," Dupree later said. He added, "And I'm kind of feeling mixed emotions. You know after 30 years, that's a hard part. Words really won't make up for what I lost. You know I lost both my parents…"

A day after his release, Dupree married his fiancée, Selma. The couple met two decades ago while he was in prison.

So consider for a moment all of your life's experiences: mundane errands, such as shopping at your local supermarket, and more significant events and milestones, such as a meaningful vacation or your school graduation. Many activities – such as going to the bank or shopping at the mall – are liberties that are taken for granted. But imagine that you no longer have the freedom to continue these daily tasks and activities. The world has changed around you.

Never stop being grateful for your freedom. In the words of the state district judge, Judge Adams, to Dupree, "You are free to go."

מִתְּחִלָּה

עוֹבְדֵי עֲבוֹדָה זָרָה הָיוּ אֲבוֹתֵינוּ,

וְעַכְשָׁיו קֵרְבָנוּ הַמָּקוֹם לַעֲבוֹדָתוֹ.
שֶׁנֶּאֱמַר: "וַיֹּאמֶר יְהוֹשֻׁעַ אֶל כָּל הָעָם:
כֹּה אָמַר יְיָ אֱלֹהֵי יִשְׂרָאֵל:
בְּעֵבֶר הַנָּהָר יָשְׁבוּ אֲבוֹתֵיכֶם מֵעוֹלָם,
תֶּרַח אֲבִי אַבְרָהָם וַאֲבִי נָחוֹר,
וַיַּעַבְדוּ אֱלֹהִים אֲחֵרִים.
וָאֶקַּח אֶת אֲבִיכֶם אֶת אַבְרָהָם
מֵעֵבֶר הַנָּהָר וָאוֹלֵךְ אוֹתוֹ בְּכָל אֶרֶץ כְּנָעַן,
אַרְבֶּה אֶת זַרְעוֹ וָאֶתֶּן לוֹ אֶת יִצְחָק.
וָאֶתֵּן לְיִצְחָק אֶת יַעֲקֹב וְאֶת עֵשָׂו,
וָאֶתֵּן לְעֵשָׂו אֶת הַר שֵׂעִיר לָרֶשֶׁת אוֹתוֹ,
וְיַעֲקֹב וּבָנָיו יָרְדוּ מִצְרָיִם".

(יהושע כ"ד ב'-ד')

Join a Group

It would appear from Tosafot that God has separate books for Mitzvot done by individuals and for Mitzvot accomplished by groups. Now, we know that when the Talmud discusses books of God, the reference is merely figurative. God has no physical body and there is no physical existence in Heaven. But the imagery of books does have meaning. It is not merely a cute description. Rather, the explanation is that when a group does a Mitzvah together, it is quite a different spiritual reality than if an individual performs a holy deed. It is not a difference of the quantity of

In the beginning
our fathers served idols;

In the beginning our fathers served idols; but now the Omnipresent One has brought us close to His service, as it is said: "Joshua said to all the people: thus said Hashem, the God of Israel, Your fathers used to live on the other side of the river – Terach, the father of Abraham and the father of Nachor, and they served other gods. And I took your father Abraham from beyond the river, and I led him throughout the whole land of Canaan. I increased his seed and gave him Isaac, and to Isaac I gave Jacob and Esau. To Esau I gave Mount Seir to possess it, and Jacob and his sons went down to Egypt." (Joshua 24:2–4)

....

> more people being involved in the action. Rather, the action is qualitatively different in the eyes of God when a group is involved. Therefore, it warrants a separate book. It deserves a separate "spiritual group file cabinet" and cannot be "filed" together with the positive actions of individuals.
>
> It has been suggested that the word "team" stands for "Together Everyone Accomplishes More." Teamwork and working as a community are not simply ways to combine individuals' achievements. Rather, the team succeeds in ways that would be unimaginable for individuals.
>
> **Rabbi Boruch Leff**

בָּרוּךְ
שׁוֹמֵר הַבְטָחָתוֹ לְיִשְׂרָאֵל, בָּרוּךְ הוּא.

שֶׁהַקָדוֹשׁ בָּרוּךְ הוּא חִשַּׁב אֶת הַקֵּץ,
לַעֲשׂוֹת כְּמָה שֶׁאָמַר לְאַבְרָהָם אָבִינוּ
בִּבְרִית בֵּין הַבְּתָרִים,
שֶׁנֶּאֱמַר: "וַיֹּאמֶר לְאַבְרָם, יָדֹעַ תֵּדַע
כִּי גֵר יִהְיֶה זַרְעֲךָ בְּאֶרֶץ לֹא לָהֶם,
וַעֲבָדוּם וְעִנּוּ אֹתָם אַרְבַּע מֵאוֹת שָׁנָה.
וְגַם אֶת הַגּוֹי אֲשֶׁר יַעֲבֹדוּ דָּן אָנֹכִי
וְאַחֲרֵי כֵן יֵצְאוּ בִּרְכֻשׁ גָּדוֹל". (בראשית ט"ו י"ג-י"ד)

Momentum

There is a wonderful story of a poor farmer who lived under the rule of a miserable poritz (landowner) in medieval Europe. The evil landowner provided minimal shelter in exchange for a large portion of the farmer's profits. The farmer and his wife toiled under the most severe conditions to support their family with a few chickens that laid eggs and a cow that gave milk. Ultimately, time took its toll and hardship became the norm. The farmer and his wife had their bitter routine and never hoped for better. One day the farmer came back from the market quite upset. "What's the matter?" cried his wife, "you look as if the worst calamity has happened." "It has," sighed the anxious farmer. "They say in the market that the Moshiach is coming. He will take us all to the land of Israel. What will be of our cow and our chickens? Where will we live? Who will provide shelter for us? Oy! What is going to be?" His wife, who was steeped with faith in the Almighty, answered calmly. "Don't worry my dear husband.

Blessed

is He who keeps His promise to Israel, blessed be He! For the Holy One, blessed be He, calculated the end [of the bondage], in order to do as He had said to our father Abraham at the "Covenant between the Portions," as it is said: "And He said to Abraham, You shall know that your seed will be strangers in a land that is not theirs, and they will enslave them and make them suffer, for four hundred years. But I shall also judge the nation whom they shall serve, and after that they will come out with great wealth.'" (Genesis 16:13–14)

The Good Lord always protects His people. He saved us from Pharaoh in Egypt, He redeemed us from the evil Haman and has protected us from harsh decrees throughout our exile. No doubt he will protect us from this Moshiach too!"

Hashem understood that the Jewish people were mired in exile for 210 years. Moshe had to be as forceful with those he was planning to redeem as he was with those who had enslaved them. Often in life, whether by choice or by chance, we enter into situations that we ought not be in. As time progresses, however, we get accustomed to the situation, and our worst enemy becomes change. We must tell the Pharaoh within each of us, "Let my people go!" Let us not continue on the comfortable path but rather get on the correct one. That message must be told to the victim in us with the same force and intensity as it is told to the complacent.

Rabbi Mordechai Kamenetzky

A Glass Half Full

When someone has helped you, but has perhaps not done all that you requested, focus on what the person has done, not on what he hasn't. Although this would seem to be morally obvious, many people are so caught up with their own wants and needs that they ignore the good done for them. Thus Rabbi Eliyahu Dessler, one of the great figures of twentieth-century Mussar, once received a letter from a student, posing fourteen unrelated questions on a variety of subjects. Rabbi Dessler wrote back a long reply in which he dealt with thirteen of the questions. His son received a return letter from the student, who not only noted the omission, but expressed no thanks for what the rabbi had written.

Though Rabbi Dessler was a man of great patience, he was pained by the student's behavior: "Not only [was there no word of thanks], but at the beginning of your letter you reminded me that there was one of your questions to which I forgot to furnish an answer… Was that the proper beginning [and response] to a letter of ten pages?" He went on to tell the

מַחֲזִירִים אֶת הַקְּעָרָה לִמְקוֹמָהּ,
מְגַלִּים אֶת שְׁלֹשׁ הַמַּצּוֹת וְאוֹמְרִים:

וְהִיא שֶׁעָמְדָה לַאֲבוֹתֵינוּ וְלָנוּ;

שֶׁלֹּא אֶחָד בִּלְבָד עָמַד עָלֵינוּ לְכַלּוֹתֵנוּ,
אֶלָּא שֶׁבְּכָל דּוֹר וָדוֹר עוֹמְדִים עָלֵינוּ לְכַלּוֹתֵנוּ,
וְהַקָּדוֹשׁ בָּרוּךְ הוּא מַצִּילֵנוּ מִיָּדָם.

· ·

Recognizing the Good

(The following story, widely circulated, has been shown not to have actually happened but regardless contains a message for all of us).

student: "(I mention this) not because I need you thanks, but because of my love for you and concern that you not become a person who denies the good done for him. Recall what I wrote… concerning the words of our Sages: "Whoever denies the good done him by his friend will in the end deny the good Hakadosh Baruch Hu (God) has done him as well."

Rabbi Joseph Telushkin

Zionism as Progress

It is manifestly right that the scattered Jews should have a national center and a national home to be re-united, and where else but in Palestine, with which for three thousand years they have been intimately and profoundly associated? We think it will be good for the world, good for the Jews, good for the British Empire, but also good for the Arabs who swell in Palestine…they shall share in the benefits and progress of Zionism.

Winston Churchill
Reply to an Arab delegation, Jerusalem, 1921

Return the Seder Plate to its place,
uncover the three Matzot and say.

This is what has stood by our fathers and us!

For not just one alone has risen against us to destroy us, but in every generation they rise against us to destroy us; and the Holy One, blessed be He, saves us from their hand!

There is a story – concerning the famous violinist Itzhak Perlman. One evening, Perlman was in New York to give a concert. As a child he had been stricken with polio and getting on stage is no small feat for him. He wears braces on both legs and walks with two crutches. Perlman crossed the stage painfully slowly, until he reached the chair in which he seated himself to play.

As soon as he appeared on stage that night, the audience applauded and then waited respectfully as he made his way slowly across the stage. He took his seat, signaled to the conductor, and began to play.

No sooner had he finished the first few bars than one of the strings on his violin snapped with a report like gunshot. At that point Perlman was close enough to the beginning of the piece that it would have been reasonable to bring the concert to a halt while he replaced the string to begin again. But that's not what he did. He waited a moment and then signaled the conductor to pick up just where they had left off.

Perlman now had only three strings with which to play his soloist part. He was able to find some of the missing notes on adjoining strings, but where that wasn't possible, he had to rearrange the music on the spot in his head so that it all still held together.

He played with passion and artistry, spontaneously rearranging the symphony right through to the end. When he finally rested his bow, the audience sat for a moment in stunned silence. And then they rose to their feet and cheered wildly. They knew they had been witness to an extraordinary display of human skill and ingenuity.

Perlman raised his bow to signal for quiet. "You know," he said, "sometimes it is the artist's task to find out how much beautiful music you can still make with what you have left."

We have to wonder, was he speaking of his violin strings or his crippled body? And is it true only for artists? We are all lacking something, and so we are all challenged to answer the question: Do we have the attitude of making something of beauty out of what we do have, incomplete as it may be?

The Hebrew term for gratitude is hakarat hatov, which means, literally, "recognizing the good." Practicing gratitude means recognizing the good that is already yours.

To what and whom should we feel thankful? In the Torah, when Moses brought the plagues onto Egypt, he wasn't the one who initiated turning the Nile River into blood and bringing frogs from the river. His brother Aaron invoked those plagues. The medieval commentator Rashi explains that since the river had protected Moses when he was an infant, he could not start a plague against it. God was teaching Moses a powerful lesson in gratitude: we can open in gratitude even to inanimate objects.

Whenever Rabbi Menachem Mendel, the Kotzker Rebbe, replaced a pair of worn out shoes, he would neatly wrap up the old ones in newspaper before placing them in the trash, and he would declare, "How can I simply toss away such a fine pair of shoes that have served me so well these past years!?" I felt the same way when I gave away my 1984 Honda that had ferried me so reliably for 18 years.

Dr. Alan Morinis

יַנִּיחַ אֶת הַכּוֹס מִיָּדוֹ וִיגַלֶּה אֶת הַמַּצּוֹת.

צֵא וּלְמַד,
מַה בִּקֵּשׁ לָבָן הָאֲרַמִּי לַעֲשׂוֹת לְיַעֲקֹב אָבִינוּ;
שֶׁפַּרְעֹה לֹא גָזַר אֶלָּא עַל הַזְּכָרִים,
וְלָבָן בִּקֵּשׁ לַעֲקוֹר אֶת הַכֹּל,
שֶׁנֶּאֱמַר:
"אֲרַמִּי אֹבֵד אָבִי וַיֵּרֶד מִצְרַיְמָה, וַיָּגָר שָׁם בִּמְתֵי מְעָט, וַיְהִי שָׁם לְגוֹי גָּדוֹל עָצוּם וָרָב". (דברים כ"ו ה')

• •

Jewish Unity – Unity Does Not Mean Conformity

In my definition of Jewish unity, I veered far away from the political. Jewish unity to me was about loving and caring about Jews all over the world. It was about being part of a beautiful whole. It wasn't about condoning or condemning. It wasn't about admiring or acquiescing. It was about the connectedness, the warmth, the knowledge that underneath it all we are one nation, responsible for one for another.

Jewish unity is about recognizing our similarities. Disunity comes from fixating on our differences. When I look at you, do I see another soul who stood with me at Sinai? Or do I see someone whose observances are dissimilar to mine, whose speech and dress are too different from my own? The more I focus on how different we are, the more I drive us apart.

◀ I had occasion to spend a Shabbat in a chassidic enclave known as Kiryas Joel. In fact, my family was hosted by our cousins who are, themselves, chassidic. We, however, although observant, are not chassidic, and our customs, dress, and even language are very different from theirs. I have to say that I felt hesitant, driving into my cousin's community. Would we feel embarrassed? Would they look down on us or try to change us?

Put down the wine cup and uncover the matzah.

Go forth and learn what Laban the Aramean wanted to do to our father Jacob. Pharaoh had issued a decree against the male children only, but Laban wanted to uproot everyone – as it is said: **"The Aramean wished to destroy my father; and he went down to Egypt and sojourned there, few in number; and he became there a nation - great and mighty and numerous."** (Deuteronomy 26:5)

One of the most uplifting, beautiful Shabbats ensued. My cousins accepted us with open arms, exactly the way we were. They accommodated us in every way possible. Other members of the community went out of their way to make us feel welcome, although we clearly stood out. And you know the funniest thing? Over the course of that Shabbat, we found out that underneath it all, we really weren't all that dissimilar. In fact, we were very much the same. We had the same struggles, the same triumphs. They also worried about peer pressure, parenting, and nuclear threats. They, too, dealt with laundry stains, expensive food bills, and infectious diseases. My long-standing convictions that chassidim were somehow unapproachable and too unlike us to even get along with, dissolved.

Jewish unity empowers us as a nation. It empowers us as individuals within the framework of a whole. It makes us stronger, better, deeper people. We just need to recognize its value and work on strengthening the bonds between us.

Riva Pomerantz

Yearning for Return

The politics of Israel at times leads us to forget what matters most. To remember, let us retell the story of Max Nordau.

Max Nordau became a leader of the Zionist movement, co founding the World Zionist Organization with Theodore Herzl. In Nordau's diaries he tell the following story:

An assimilated Vienna physician, Nordau once treated an indigent family, saving the life of their 12 year-old girls. Knowing she could not pay him, he said he would take a kiss as payment. She said that as a religious girl she could not kiss a grown man. So he asked her instead to pay him with the Torah lesson she had learned this morning. The girl recounted

"וַיֵּרֶד מִצְרַיְמָה", אָנוּס עַל פִּי הַדִּבּוּר. "וַיָּגָר שָׁם", מְלַמֵּד שֶׁלֹּא יָרַד יַעֲקֹב אָבִינוּ לְהִשְׁתַּקֵּעַ בְּמִצְרַיִם אֶלָּא לָגוּר שָׁם, שֶׁנֶּאֱמַר: "וַיֹּאמְרוּ אֶל פַּרְעֹה, לָגוּר בָּאָרֶץ בָּאנוּ, כִּי אֵין מִרְעֶה לַצֹּאן אֲשֶׁר לַעֲבָדֶיךָ, כִּי כָבֵד הָרָעָב בְּאֶרֶץ כְּנָעַן. וְעַתָּה יֵשְׁבוּ נָא עֲבָדֶיךָ בְּאֶרֶץ גֹּשֶׁן".
(בראשית מ"ז ד') "בִּמְתֵי מְעָט", כְּמָה שֶׁנֶּאֱמַר: "בְּשִׁבְעִים נֶפֶשׁ יָרְדוּ אֲבוֹתֶיךָ מִצְרָיְמָה, וְעַתָּה שָׂמְךָ יְיָ אֱלֹהֶיךָ כְּכוֹכְבֵי הַשָּׁמַיִם לָרֹב". (דברים י' כ"ב) "וַיְהִי שָׁם לְגוֹי", מְלַמֵּד שֶׁהָיוּ יִשְׂרָאֵל מְצֻיָּנִים שָׁם.

Invictus

One Out of the night that covers me,
Black as the Pit from pole to pole,
I thank whatever gods may be
For my unconquerable soul.

In the fell clutch of circumstance
I have not winced nor cried aloud.
Under the bludgeonings of chance
My head is bloody, but unbowed.

> the tale of Jacobs's choosing not to walk the 20 miles to bury Rachel in Meorat Hamachpelah, the traditional burial Cave of the patriarchs. She was buried instead at the side of the road. Our rabbis teach, the girl told Nordau, that Jacob made that choice so that when the Jews went into exile as they passed by her tomb, "Rachel would weep for her children" (Jeremiah 31:15,16)
>
> Nordau wrote in his diary that if after 2000 years of exile Jewish children still learned about returning to Israel, it would certainly come to pass.
>
> **Rabbi David Wolpe**
> Jewish Week May 21, 2010

"And he went down to Egypt" forced by Divine decree. **"And he sojourned there"** this teaches that our father Jacob did not go down to Egypt to settle, but only to live there temporarily. Thus it is said, "They said to Pharaoh, We have come to sojourn in the land, for there is no pasture for your servants' flocks because the hunger is severe in the land of Canaan; and now, please, let your servants dwell in the land of Goshen." (Genesis 47:4) **"Few in number"** as it is said: "Your fathers went down to Egypt with seventy persons, and now, Hashem, your God, has made you as numerous as the stars of heaven." (Deuteronomy 10:22) **"There he became a nation"** this teaches that Israel was distinctive there.

Beyond this place of wrath and tears
Looms but the Horror of the shade,
And yet the menace of the years
Finds, and shall find, me unafraid.

It matters not how strait the gate,
How charged with punishments the scroll.
I am the master of my fate:
I am the captain of my soul.

William Ernest Henley (August 23, 1849 - July 11, 1903) was a British poet, critic and editor.

After suffering tuberculosis as a boy, he found himself, in 1874, aged twenty-five, an inmate of the hospital at Edinburgh. From there he sent to the Cornhill Magazine where he wrote poems in irregular rhythms, describing with poignant force his experiences in hospital. (So Mr. Henley was redeemed, as it were, from a chronic illness).

Nelson Mandela was an anti-apartheid activist, and the leader of the African National Congress's armed wing Umkhonto we Sizwe. The "Judiciary of South Africa" South African courts convicted him on charges of sabotage, as well as other crimes committed while he led the movement against apartheid. In accordance with his conviction, Mr. Mandela served 27 years in prison. Following his release from prison on 11 February 1990, Mr. Mandela supported reconciliation and negotiation, and helped lead the transition towards multi-racial democracy in South Africa. Nelson Mandela had the above poem written on a scrap of paper on his prison cell wall while he was incarcerated.

・・・

"גָּדוֹל עָצוּם", כְּמָה שֶׁנֶּאֱמַר: "וּבְנֵי יִשְׂרָאֵל פָּרוּ וַיִּשְׁרְצוּ וַיִּרְבּוּ וַיַּעַצְמוּ בִּמְאֹד מְאֹד, וַתִּמָּלֵא הָאָרֶץ אֹתָם". (שמות א' ז') "וָרָב", כְּמָה שֶׁנֶּאֱמַר: "רְבָבָה כְּצֶמַח הַשָּׂדֶה נְתַתִּיךְ, וַתִּרְבִּי וַתִּגְדְּלִי וַתָּבֹאִי בַּעֲדִי עֲדָיִים, שָׁדַיִם נָכֹנוּ וּשְׂעָרֵךְ צִמֵּחַ, וְאַתְּ עֵרֹם וְעֶרְיָה". (יחזקאל ט"ז, ו') "וָאֶעֱבֹר עָלַיִךְ וָאֶרְאֵךְ מִתְבּוֹסֶסֶת בְּדָמָיִךְ, וָאֹמַר לָךְ בְּדָמַיִךְ חֲיִי, וָאֹמַר לָךְ בְּדָמַיִךְ חֲיִי". (יחזקאל ט"ז, ז')

・・・

For Those Who Came Before Us

Let us raise above our highest joy
The memory of all those

I Must Become We

Yes, my great-grandparents and not me myself left Egypt; but in an existential sense I left with them because I identify with them, because I have transformed the past historical-national memory of the servitude and the exodus into part of my own personal present-day life experience. A single individual, no matter how intelligent or powerful, is limited in time and ability; the Jewish nation is eternal, with eternal values dedicated to redeeming the world – in no small measure based upon lessons concerning human freedom and individual dignity gleaned from the paschal sacrifice. Insofar as an individual identifies with his Jewish past, he/she participates in eternity. And only those who identify with their past will contribute to – and be part of – a future beyond themselves. In order to be plugged into eternity, your "I" must become a "we", you must plug yourself into our national-historical rituals and traditions. Only by going beyond yourself will you ultimately guarantee your future!

Rabbi Riskin

"**Great, mighty,**" as it is said: "And the children of Israel were fruitful and increased abundantly, and multiplied and became very, very mighty, and the land became filled with them." (Exodus 1:7) "**And numerous,**" as it is said: "I caused you to thrive like the plants of the field, and you increased and grew and became very beautiful, your bosom fashioned and your hair grown long, but you were still naked. (Ezekiel 16:7) I passed over you wallowing in your blood, and I said to you 'By your blood you shall live' and I said to you 'By your blood you shall live!'" (Ezekiel 16:6)

Whose blood as spilled
over the foundation stones
Of our political liberation,
for with their death
They bequeathed life to us.

"And when I...saw thee wallowing in thy blood,
I said unto thee: In thy blood, live." Ezekiel 16:6

"Oh that my head were waters,
And mine eyes a fountain of tears,
That I might weep day and night
for the slain of the daughter of my people!"   Jeremiah 8:22

The above was a excerpt from the Haggadah of 1949 of the kibbutz Ne'ot Mordechai, in northern Israel, that was founded in 1946. It was included as a tribute to those who fell in the War of Independence 1948.

וַיָּרֵעוּ אֹתָנוּ הַמִּצְרִים וַיְעַנּוּנוּ,
וַיִּתְּנוּ עָלֵינוּ עֲבֹדָה קָשָׁה. (דברים כ"ו ו')

"וַיָּרֵעוּ אֹתָנוּ הַמִּצְרִים",
כְּמָה שֶׁנֶּאֱמַר: "הָבָה נִתְחַכְּמָה לוֹ, פֶּן יִרְבֶּה,
וְהָיָה כִּי תִקְרֶאנָה מִלְחָמָה
וְנוֹסַף גַּם הוּא עַל שֹׂנְאֵינוּ, וְנִלְחַם בָּנוּ,
וְעָלָה מִן הָאָרֶץ". (שמות א' י')

A Group Is Mandated by Law

In the Talmud's discussion of the Paschal lamb, which is to be slaughtered Passover Eve and then consumed together as a group, it used the word "*Chavurah*." The root of this word is *chaber* – to be bound or joined together. This group was just one of many small communities, all committed and bound to the same act.

Commitment is an apt word; by killing a lamb, which was considered by their Egyptian neighbors to be sacred, the Jews were launching a rebellion. They automatically distinguished themselves from those around them, and became a distinct group.

Rabbi Joseph Soloveitchik observes that on this first Passover night, God judged the Jews as a group, rather than individually. On that fateful night with the *Chavurah* groups sequestered in their homes, the doors marked by blood and the demise of the firstborn Egyptians all around them in the still darkness, either you were part of the community or you were not.

"The Egyptians treated us badly and they made us suffer, and they put hard work upon us."

(Deuteronomy 26:6)

"The Egyptians treated us badly," as it is said: Come, let us act cunningly with [the people] lest they multiply and, if there should be a war against us, they will join our enemies, fight against us and leave the land. (Exodus 1:10)

Overcoming Suffering

"If God had not brought our forefathers out of Egypt, then we, our children and our children's children would still be slaves to Pharaoh in Egypt." What a strange statement. The Pharaoh has long ceased to exist. How could we still be his slaves? Clearly, this sentence is allegorical. Pharaohs are not necessarily Egyptian. And Egypt is not the only place where exile is felt. Each generation has its own enemies, its own struggles and – sometimes – its own victories. We evoke Exodus not only to remember our suffering in Egypt, but also to relive the manner in which we overcame our suffering.

Elie Wiesel

"Neighborhood Bully"

Well, the neighborhood bully, he's just one man,
His enemies say he's on their land.
They got him outnumbered about a million to one,
He got no place to escape to, no place to run.
He's the neighborhood bully.
The neighborhood bully been driven out of every land,
He's wandered the earth an exiled man.
Seen his family scattered, his people hounded and torn,
He's always on trial for just being born.
He's the neighborhood bully.
Well, he knocked out a lynch mob, he was criticized,
Old women condemned him, said he should apologize.
Then he destroyed a bomb factory, nobody was glad.
The bombs were meant for him.
He was supposed to feel bad.
He's the neighborhood bully.
Every empire that's enslaved him is gone,
Egypt and Rome, even the great Babylon.
He's made a garden of paradise in the desert sand,

In bed with nobody, under no one's command.
He's the neighborhood bully.
Now his holiest books have been trampled upon,
No contract he signed was worth what it was written on.
He took the crumbs of the world and he turned it into wealth,
Took sickness and disease and he turned it into health.
He's the neighborhood bully.
What's anybody indebted to him for?
Nothin', they say.
He just likes to cause war.
Pride and prejudice and superstition indeed,
They wait for this bully like a dog waits to feed.
He's the neighborhood bully.
What has he done to wear so many scars?
Does he change the course of rivers?
Does he pollute the moon and stars?
Neighborhood bully, standing on the hill,
Running out the clock, time standing still,
Neighborhood bully.

Lyrics by Bob Dylan

"וַיְעַנּוּנוּ", כְּמָה שֶׁנֶּאֱמַר:
"וַיָּשִׂימוּ עָלָיו שָׂרֵי מִסִּים לְמַעַן עַנֹּתוֹ בְּסִבְלֹתָם,
וַיִּבֶן עָרֵי מִסְכְּנוֹת לְפַרְעֹה, אֶת פִּתֹם וְאֶת רַעַמְסֵס".
(שמות א' י"א)

Be Thankful

Be thankful that you don't already have everything you desire,
If you did, what would there be to look forward to?

Be thankful when you don't know something
For it gives you the opportunity to learn.

Be thankful for the difficult times.
During those times you grow.

Be thankful for your limitations
Because they give you opportunities for improvement.

Be thankful for each new challenge
Because it will build your strength and character.

Be thankful for your mistakes
They will teach you valuable lessons.

"וַיִּתְּנוּ עָלֵינוּ עֲבֹדָה קָשָׁה", כְּמָה שֶׁנֶּאֱמַר:
"וַיַּעֲבִדוּ מִצְרַיִם אֶת בְּנֵי יִשְׂרָאֵל בְּפָרֶךְ". (שמות א' י"ג)

**וַנִּצְעַק אֶל יְיָ אֱלֹהֵי אֲבֹתֵינוּ, וַיִּשְׁמַע יְיָ אֶת קֹלֵנוּ,
וַיַּרְא אֶת עָנְיֵנוּ וְאֶת עֲמָלֵנוּ וְאֶת לַחֲצֵנוּ.** (דברים כ"ו ז')

"And they made us suffer," as it is said: "They set taskmasters over [the people of Israel] to make them suffer with their burdens, and they built storage cities for Pharaoh, Pitom and Ramses."

(Exodus 1:11)

Be thankful when you're tired and weary
Because it means you've made a difference.

It is easy to be thankful for the good things.
A life of rich fulfillment comes to those who are
also thankful for the setbacks.

GRATITUDE can turn a negative into a positive.
Find a way to be thankful for your troubles
and they can become your blessings.

Anonymous

"And they put hard work upon us," as it is said: "The Egyptians made the children of Israel work with rigor. And they made their lives bitter with hard work, with mortar and with bricks and all manner of service in the field, all their work which they made them work with rigor." (Exodus 1:13)

"And we cried out to Hashem, the God of our fathers, and the God heard our voice and saw our suffering, our labor and our oppression." (Deuteronomy 26:7)

Transforming the Past

Resh Lakish said that repentance is so great that premeditated sins are accounted as though they were mitzvot (merits) (Talmud Bavli Yoma 86b).

How can an *aveira* – a sin – be transformed into a *mitzva*?

Rabbi Soliveitchik writes in his book *Halakhic Man* that when one looks to improve oneself – call it repentance – one first looks upon the past and determines what has occurred and what might still be occurring. Next, one thinks about the future and distinguishes between a future that is on the way to be completed versus a future that has yet to be created. Finally, one considers the causes located in the past in light of the future and determines its direction and destination.

The main principle is that the future should dominate the past and reign over it. Our past shortcomings can be transformed underneath the

"וַנִּצְעַק אֶל יְיָ אֱלֹהֵי אֲבֹתֵינוּ", כְּמָה שֶׁנֶּאֱמַר: "וַיְהִי בַיָּמִים הָרַבִּים הָהֵם וַיָּמָת מֶלֶךְ מִצְרַיִם, וַיֵּאָנְחוּ בְנֵי יִשְׂרָאֵל מִן הָעֲבוֹדָה וַיִּזְעָקוּ, וַתַּעַל שַׁוְעָתָם אֶל הָאֱלֹהִים מִן הָעֲבֹדָה". (שמות ב' כ"ג) **"וַיִּשְׁמַע יְיָ אֶת־קֹלֵנוּ"**, כְּמָה שֶׁנֶּאֱמַר: "וַיִּשְׁמַע אֱלֹהִים אֶת נַאֲקָתָם, וַיִּזְכֹּר אֱלֹהִים אֶת בְּרִיתוֹ אֶת אַבְרָהָם, אֶת יִצְחָק וְאֶת יַעֲקֹב". (שמות ב' כ"ד) **"וַיַּרְא אֶת עָנְיֵנוּ"**, זוֹ פְּרִישׁוּת דֶּרֶךְ אֶרֶץ, כְּמָה שֶׁנֶּאֱמַר: "וַיַּרְא אֱלֹהִים אֶת בְּנֵי יִשְׂרָאֵל וַיֵּדַע אֱלֹהִים". (שמות ב' כ"ה) **"וְאֶת עֲמָלֵנוּ"**, אֵלּוּ הַבָּנִים, כְּמָה שֶׁנֶּאֱמַר: "כָּל הַבֵּן הַיִּלּוֹד הַיְאֹרָה תַּשְׁלִיכֻהוּ וְכָל הַבַּת תְּחַיּוּן". (שמות א' כ"ב) **"וְאֶת לַחֲצֵנוּ"**, זֶה הַדְּחַק, כְּמָה שֶׁנֶּאֱמַר: "וְגַם רָאִיתִי אֶת הַלַּחַץ אֲשֶׁר מִצְרַיִם לֹחֲצִים אֹתָם". (שמות ג' ט')

guiding hand of the future into a source of merit and good deeds.

Our past becomes a learning experience, as Rabbi Chaim Navon observes about two people who are involved in a traffic accident. This incident, now in the past for these two individuals, will be reflected upon, and there are at least two possible outcomes. One can decide not to drive again or one can build upon that experience to become a more careful driver and better still, to influence others to drive more carefully.

One can dwell in the past indefinitely or one can use the past to transform what has occurred into building blocks of a better tomorrow.

"And we cried out to Hashem, the God of our fathers," as it is said: "During that long period, the king of Egypt died; and the children of Israel groaned because of the servitude, and they cried out. And their cry for help from their servitude rose up to God." (Exodus 2:23) **"And Hashem heard our voice"** as it said: "And God heard their groaning, and God remembered His covenant with Abraham, Isaac and Jacob." (Exodus 2:24) **"And he saw our suffering"** this refers to the separation of husband and wife, as it is said: "God saw the children of Israel and God took note." (Exodus 2:25) **"Our labor,"** this refers to the "children," as it is said: "Every boy that is born, you shall throw into the river and every girl you shall keep alive." (Exodus 2:22) **"And our oppression,"** this refers to the pressure, as it is said: "I have seen the oppression with which the Egyptians oppress them." (Exodus 3:9)

וַיּוֹצִאֵנוּ יְיָ מִמִּצְרַיִם בְּיָד חֲזָקָה וּבִזְרֹעַ נְטוּיָה, וּבְמֹרָא גָּדֹל, וּבְאֹתוֹת וּבְמֹפְתִים. (דברים כ״ו ח׳)

"וַיּוֹצִאֵנוּ יְיָ מִמִּצְרַיִם", לֹא עַל־יְדֵי מַלְאָךְ, וְלֹא עַל־יְדֵי שָׂרָף, וְלֹא עַל־יְדֵי שָׁלִיחַ, אֶלָּא הַקָּדוֹשׁ בָּרוּךְ הוּא בִּכְבוֹדוֹ וּבְעַצְמוֹ. שֶׁנֶּאֱמַר: "וְעָבַרְתִּי בְאֶרֶץ מִצְרַיִם בַּלַּיְלָה הַזֶּה, וְהִכֵּיתִי כָל בְּכוֹר בְּאֶרֶץ מִצְרַיִם מֵאָדָם וְעַד בְּהֵמָה, וּבְכָל אֱלֹהֵי מִצְרַיִם אֶעֱשֶׂה שְׁפָטִים, אֲנִי יְיָ". (שמות י״ב י״ב)

True Gratitude

There are people who have helped you enormously in the past in one way or another. And when they gave you their assistance – whatever it might have been – you certainly expressed your gratitude. But as time went on, it's just not natural to continue to shower the person with appreciation and gratitude.

But this doesn't mean that you can't let them know "out of the blue" once again just how much you appreciate what they did for you. Saying "thank you" to the person long after they've given you their help, is such a beautiful and selfless way to live. And the recipient will appreciate it beyond words.

It is very easy to forget people who were there for us, because once their assistance is no longer needed, our appreciation for what they did can easily fade away. And as more and more time passes, we can actually

> "The God took as out of Egypt with a strong hand and an outstretched arm, and with a great manifestation, and with signs and wonders."
>
> (Deuteronomy 26:8)

"God took us out of Egypt," not through an angel, not through a seraph and not through a messenger. The Holy One, blessed be He, did it in His glory by Himself! Thus it is said: "In that night I will pass through the land of Egypt, and I will smite every first-born in the land of Egypt, from man to beast, and I will carry out judgments against all the gods of Egypt, I the God." (Exodus 12:12)

---

completely forget those people who were there for us when we needed them the most.

It's not that hard to show appreciation toward someone right after he's helped you. But the true measure of a person is not demonstrated by the gratitude you show a person after he's helped you. Rather, the measure of a person is demonstrated by the heartfelt gratitude he can still show long after the fact. True gratitude is not defined by a person who doesn't forget; it's defined by the one who always remembers. Make the call today.

Adam Lieberman

"וְעָבַרְתִּי בְאֶרֶץ מִצְרַיִם בַּלַּיְלָה הַזֶּה", אֲנִי וְלֹא מַלְאָךְ. "וְהִכֵּיתִי כָל בְּכוֹר בְּאֶרֶץ מִצְרַיִם", אֲנִי וְלֹא שָׂרָף. "וּבְכָל אֱלֹהֵי מִצְרַיִם אֶעֱשֶׂה שְׁפָטִים", אֲנִי וְלֹא הַשָּׁלִיחַ. "אֲנִי יְיָ", אֲנִי הוּא וְלֹא אַחֵר.

"בְּיָד חֲזָקָה", זוֹ הַדֶּבֶר, כְּמָה שֶׁנֶּאֱמַר: "הִנֵּה יַד יְיָ הוֹיָה בְּמִקְנְךָ אֲשֶׁר בַּשָּׂדֶה, בַּסּוּסִים, בַּחֲמֹרִים, בַּגְּמַלִּים, בַּבָּקָר וּבַצֹּאן, דֶּבֶר כָּבֵד מְאֹד". (שמות ט' ג') "וּבִזְרֹעַ נְטוּיָה", זוֹ הַחֶרֶב, כְּמָה שֶׁנֶּאֱמַר: "וְחַרְבּוֹ שְׁלוּפָה בְּיָדוֹ, נְטוּיָה עַל יְרוּשָׁלָיִם". (דברי הימים א' כ"א ט"ז) "וּבְמוֹרָא גָּדֹל", זוֹ גִּלּוּי שְׁכִינָה, כְּמָה שֶׁנֶּאֱמַר: "אוֹ הֲנִסָּה אֱלֹהִים לָבֹא לָקַחַת לוֹ גוֹי מִקֶּרֶב גּוֹי בְּמַסֹּת בְּאֹתֹת וּבְמוֹפְתִים, וּבְמִלְחָמָה וּבְיָד חֲזָקָה וּבִזְרוֹעַ נְטוּיָה, וּבְמוֹרָאִים גְּדֹלִים, כְּכֹל אֲשֶׁר עָשָׂה לָכֶם יְיָ אֱלֹהֵיכֶם בְּמִצְרַיִם לְעֵינֶיךָ". (דברים ד' ל"ד)

"I will pass through the land of Egypt," I and not an angel; **"And I will smite every first-born in the land of Egypt,"** I and not a seraph; **"And I will carry out judgments against all the gods of Egypt,"** I and not a messenger; **"I – Hashem,"** it is I, and none other! **"With a strong hand,"** this refers to the dever (pestilence) as it is said: "Behold, the hand of the God will be upon your livestock in the field, upon the horses, the donkeys, the camels, the herds and the flocks, a very severe pestilence." (Exodus 9:3) **"And with an outstretched arm,"** this refers to the sword, as it is said: "His sword was drawn, in his hand, stretched out over Jerusalem." (Chronicles 1, 1:21) **"And with a great manifestation,"** this refers to the revelation of the Shechinah (Divine Presence), as it is said: "Has any God ever tried to take for himself a nation from the midst of another nation, with trials, signs and wonders, with war and with a strong hand and an outstretched arm, and with great manifestations, like all that Hashem your God did for you in Egypt before your eyes!" (Deuteronomy 9:3)

"**וּבְאֹתֹת**", זֶה הַמַּטֶּה, כְּמָה שֶׁנֶּאֱמַר: "וְאֶת הַמַּטֶּה הַזֶּה תִּקַּח בְּיָדֶךָ, אֲשֶׁר תַּעֲשֶׂה בּוֹ אֶת הָאֹתֹת".

(שמות ד' י"ז)

Obstacles to Transformation Can be Overcome

Joel Mandel and Julius Rosenzweig have a large electrical supply house in Long Island City, NY. Their vast warehouse occupies over a million cubic feet of space containing thousands of different electrical components, from transformers as large as the average-size garage to tiny cathodes that could dance on the head of a pin.

It was a couple of years ago when some electrical doo-dad, that seemed to be a vital organ of one of my children's battery-operated what-nots, went on the blink. With zero electrical know-how, I decided to bring the component to my friends at Globe Electrical Supply and maybe they could find me a replacement.

Weaving my way through a labyrinth of shelves, boxes, and drawers, I climbed some metal steps and made my way to the old office that appeared out of a 1950s Hollywood set. An old wooden desk was the pedestal for a dusty computer that probably strained harder than their human principals to maintain the vast inventory. I showed the part to Joel, who looked at the tiny part and smiled. He called over one of the workers, "Warren," he said, "please get the rabbi a…" I couldn't make out the exact name, but it sounded like flux-capacitator, though I highly doubt that my kid's toy was dying for lack of a lack of a flux-capacitator!

Like a Tomahawk missile directed toward a predestined mark, Warren took the injured electrical component, weaved through the myriad rooms, the barrage of boxes, and an almost unlimited array of electrical paraphernalia.

Homing in on the exact location, Warren scaled a ladder that looked as if it could have been used to wash the windows of a Manhattan skyscraper, and about 30 feet off the ground, with amazing agility and

> **"And with signs,"** this refers to the staff, as it is said: "Take into your hand this staff with which you shall perform the signs." (Exodus 4:17)

precise guidance, he reached for his target – a small cardboard box. Its edges were yellowed with age, but I knew it had not been touched in five years. He placed his hand into the box and plucked out a component, which exactly matched my broken one.

As if he had rehearsed this scene from the day he started working, he held the component between his thumb and forefinger, then smiled, opened the human vise, letting the piece drop into my palm. "Here's the sucker!"

Stunned at both the accuracy and speed of the retrieval, I reacted as if I had just seen a minor miracle. "Warren!" I exclaimed, "how'd you do that?"

"Do what?" he asked with a shrug.

"Do what?" I repeated with an air of incredulity. "You just found a microscopic part hidden like a needle in all the hay in Kansas! And you knew exactly where it was."

Warren just shrugged. "I didn't do nothin' special. That's my job!"

When a person understands his mission, no portion of its fulfillment merits undue emotion. In Pirkei Avos, 2:9 Rabbi Yochanan ben Zakai tells us, "If you have learned much Torah, do not pride yourself in it, for this is the purpose for which you were created." If a person thinks "that's my job" about his every good deed, if his mission is clearly mapped in front of him, then many obstacles become less significant, more easily overcome and more likely to be ignored because after all, they are in fact all in a day's work.

Rabbi Mordechai Kamenetzky

"וּבְמֹפְתִים" זֶה הַדָּם, כְּמָה שֶׁנֶּאֱמַר: "וְנָתַתִּי מוֹפְתִים בַּשָּׁמַיִם וּבָאָרֶץ"

נוֹהֲגִים לְהַטִּיף מְעַט מִן הַכּוֹס בַּאֲמִירַת דָּם וָאֵשׁ וכו', וּבַאֲמִירַת דַּם צְפַרְדֵּעַ וכו', וּבַאֲמִירַת עֶשֶׂר הַמַּכּוֹת דְּצַ"ךְ עֲדַ"שׁ בְּאַחַ"ב וכו'.

דָּם וָאֵשׁ וְתִימְרוֹת עָשָׁן"
(יואל ג' ג')

דָּבָר אַחֵר: "בְּיָד חֲזָקָה" שְׁתַּיִם, "וּבִזְרֹעַ נְטוּיָה" שְׁתַּיִם, "וּבְמֹרָא גָּדֹל" שְׁתַּיִם, "וּבְאֹתוֹת" שְׁתַּיִם, "וּבְמֹפְתִים" שְׁתַּיִם.

אֵלּוּ עֶשֶׂר מַכּוֹת שֶׁהֵבִיא הַקָּדוֹשׁ בָּרוּךְ הוּא עַל־הַמִּצְרִים בְּמִצְרַיִם, וְאֵלּוּ הֵן:

דָּם, צְפַרְדֵּעַ, כִּנִּים, עָרוֹב, דֶּבֶר, שְׁחִין, בָּרָד, אַרְבֶּה, חֹשֶׁךְ, מַכַּת בְּכוֹרוֹת.

רַבִּי יְהוּדָה הָיָה נוֹתֵן בָּהֶם סִמָּנִים:

דְּצַ"ךְ עֲדַ"שׁ בְּאַחַ"ב.

"And wonders," this refers to the blood, as it is said: "And I shall show wonders in heaven and on earth.

<small>It is customary to drop or spill a few drops of wine from one's wine glass as one says "Blood, and fire"… and similarly to drop or spill a few drops of wine when mentioning each of the ten plagues, "Blood, frogs …" and again to spill a minute amount when saying the acronyms "DeTzaCh…"</small>

Blood, and fire, and pillars of smoke (Joel 3,3)

Another explanation: **"Strong hand"** indicates two [plagues]; **"Outstretched arm,"** another two; **"Great manifestation,"** another two; **"Signs,"** another two; and **"Wonders,"** another two.

These are the Ten Plagues which the Holy One, blessed be He, brought upon the Egyptians, namely as follows:

**Blood. Frogs. Lice.
Wild Beasts. Pestilence. Boils. Hail.
Locust. Darkness. Slaying of the First-born.**

Rabbi Yehudah referred to them by acronyms

DeTzaCh (blood, frogs, lice);
ADaSh (beasts, pestilence, boils);
BeAChaV (hail, locust, darkness, first-born).

רַבִּי יוֹסֵי הַגְּלִילִי אוֹמֵר: מִנַּיִן אַתָּה אוֹמֵר שֶׁלָּקוּ הַמִּצְרִים בְּמִצְרַיִם עֶשֶׂר מַכּוֹת, וְעַל הַיָּם לָקוּ חֲמִשִּׁים מַכּוֹת? בְּמִצְרַיִם מָה הוּא אוֹמֵר? "וַיֹּאמְרוּ הַחַרְטֻמִּים אֶל פַּרְעֹה: אֶצְבַּע אֱלֹהִים הִיא". (שמות ח' ט"ו) וְעַל הַיָּם מָה הוּא אוֹמֵר? "וַיַּרְא יִשְׂרָאֵל אֶת הַיָּד הַגְּדֹלָה אֲשֶׁר עָשָׂה יְיָ בְּמִצְרַיִם, וַיִּירְאוּ הָעָם אֶת יְיָ, וַיַּאֲמִינוּ בַּייָ וּבְמֹשֶׁה עַבְדּוֹ". (שמות י"ד ל"א) כַּמָּה לָקוּ בְאֶצְבַּע? עֶשֶׂר מַכּוֹת. אֱמֹר מֵעַתָּה: בְּמִצְרַיִם לָקוּ עֶשֶׂר מַכּוֹת, וְעַל הַיָּם לָקוּ חֲמִשִּׁים מַכּוֹת.

רַבִּי אֱלִיעֶזֶר אוֹמֵר: מִנַּיִן שֶׁכָּל מַכָּה וּמַכָּה שֶׁהֵבִיא הַקָּדוֹשׁ בָּרוּךְ הוּא עַל הַמִּצְרִים בְּמִצְרַיִם, הָיְתָה שֶׁל אַרְבַּע מַכּוֹת? שֶׁנֶּאֱמַר: **"יְשַׁלַּח בָּם חֲרוֹן אַפּוֹ, עֶבְרָה וָזַעַם וְצָרָה, מִשְׁלַחַת מַלְאֲכֵי רָעִים".** (תהלים ע"ח מ"ט) "עֶבְרָה" אַחַת, "וָזַעַם" שְׁתַּיִם, "וְצָרָה" שָׁלֹשׁ, "מִשְׁלַחַת מַלְאֲכֵי רָעִים" אַרְבַּע. אֱמֹר מֵעַתָּה: "בְּמִצְרַיִם לָקוּ אַרְבָּעִים מַכּוֹת, וְעַל הַיָּם לָקוּ מָאתַיִם מַכּוֹת.

Rabbi Yosi the Gallilean said: How do you know that the Egyptians were stricken by ten plagues in Egypt, and then were struck by fifty plagues at the sea? In Egypt it says of them, "The magicians said to Pharaoh 'This is the finger of God.'" (Exodus 8:16) At the sea it says, "Israel saw the great hand that Hashem laid against Egypt; and the people feared Hashem, and they believed in the God and in His servant Moses." (Exodus 14:31) Now, how often were they smitten by 'the finger'? Ten plagues! Thus you must conclude that in Egypt they were smitten by ten plagues, at the sea they were smitten by fifty plagues!

Rabbi Eliezer said: How do we know that each individual plague which the Holy One, blessed be He, brought upon the Egyptians in Egypt consisted of four plagues? For it is said: **"He sent against them His fierce anger, fury, and indignation, and trouble, a discharge of messengers of evil":** (Psalms 78:49) Fury, is one; Indignation, makes two; Trouble, makes three; Discharge of messengers of evil, makes four. Thus you must now say that in Egypt they were struck by forty plagues, and at the sea they were stricken by two hundred plagues.

רַבִּי עֲקִיבָא אוֹמֵר: מִנַּיִן שֶׁכָּל מַכָּה וּמַכָּה שֶׁהֵבִיא הַקָּדוֹשׁ בָּרוּךְ הוּא עַל הַמִּצְרִים בְּמִצְרַיִם, הָיְתָה שֶׁל חָמֵשׁ מַכּוֹת? שֶׁנֶּאֱמַר: "יְשַׁלַּח בָּם חֲרוֹן אַפּוֹ, עֶבְרָה וָזַעַם וְצָרָה, מִשְׁלַחַת מַלְאֲכֵי רָעִים". (תהלים ע"ח מ"ט)
"חֲרוֹן אַפּוֹ" אַחַת, "עֶבְרָה" שְׁתַּיִם, "וָזַעַם" שָׁלֹשׁ, "וְצָרָה" אַרְבַּע, "מִשְׁלַחַת מַלְאֲכֵי רָעִים" חָמֵשׁ. אֱמוֹר מֵעַתָּה: בְּמִצְרַיִם לָקוּ חֲמִשִּׁים מַכּוֹת וְעַל הַיָּם לָקוּ חֲמִשִּׁים וּמָאתַיִם מַכּוֹת.

• •

Concepts of Freedom - Approach #2:
Enslaved to Our Personalities

Possessed within man is an innermost will which above all else desires to be decent and holy. Deep down, every single one of us would like to be a compassionate, kind, and caring human being. We would like to have lofty and spiritual values in place of indulging in materialism and devoting our lives to the pursuit of money, power, and celebrity. We crave to be the kind of individuals who, upon leaving a gathering of friends, can feel confident that our peers have only kind things to speak of us. What we really want to be is charitable, offering compliments freely and showing appreciation to family, friends, rather than being envious of their success. We wish to be totally devoted to our spouse and the finest parents

Rabbi Akiva said: How do we know that each individual plague which the Holy One, blessed be He, brought upon the Egyptians in Egypt consisted of five plagues? For it is said: **"He sent against them his fierce anger, fury, and indignation, and trouble, a discharge of messengers of evil"**: (Psalms 78:49) **"His fierce anger,"** is one; **"fury"** makes two; **"indignation"** makes three; **"trouble"** makes four; **"discharge of messengers of evil"** makes five. Thus you must now say that in Egypt they were struck by fifty plagues, and at the sea they were stricken by two hundred and fifty plagues.

---

that the world has ever seen. We seek to be diplomatic and gracious in all social interactions, never losing our temper or offering an unkind word or opinion. Is there anyone reading this essay whose life's aspirations do not include all the above? One day when you have passed from this earth, do you wish to remembered as successful, or charitable? Does anyone care to be eulogized by a Rabbi as having owned ten apartment blocks, or having had time for everyone in need? And if we want this so badly, why doesn't it just happen? Because we are slaves to our nature.

Rabbi Shmuley Boteach

כַּמָּה מַעֲלוֹת טוֹבוֹת לַמָּקוֹם עָלֵינוּ!

The Jewish Gratitude Blessing

Four categories of people should express particular gratitude to God:

Those who have completed sea voyages,
Those who have arrived at settlements after passing through the desert,
Those who have recovered from an illness, and
Those who have been freed from prison . . .

What is the blessing they recite? Hagomel.

Blessed are You, Lord our God,
Ruler of the universe,
Who is gracious even to those who may not be worthy --
You have graciously extended great kindness to me.

But "freed from prison?" Definitely! I have spoken on behalf of my fellowship once at a prison, and with God's help I will do so again. And I will tell you the three "revelations" that experience gave me.

Number one, that it is only because "recovery" caught me before the police did, that I was enabled to be sitting on the other side of the room that night. Looking back, there were more than a few close encounters with the law and incriminating circumstances that could easily have led to a different sort of "time."

How many levels of favors has the Omnipresent One bestowed upon us:

Number two, I found that I had at least as much in common with my brother addicts in prison as I do with my fellow congregants at a Shabbat morning kiddush – maybe even more, as we recovering addicts are no longer so socially inclined to leave out the bad stuff. One of the more significant spiritual lessons I have learned in my recovery is to look beyond appearances and to realize that, especially in matters of the heart and soul, most people have more in common than the history of human intolerance would ever suggest.

But the most exhilarating discovery of all was how great it feels to walk out of a prison and not be stopped! Joni Mitchell's wise observation – that you never know what you've got until it's gone (or until you're this close to losing it) – remains as true as ever. Indeed, that recollection of being on the precipice of losing it all is a powerful motivator of many an addict's recovery – and continuing gratitude.

And what does it mean to be freed from prison? To feel a giddy and a bit more alive and vibrant. To be willing and able to take some time to stop and smell the roses, watch the sun set, or head over to a meeting. And most of all – to have choices, choices that always seemed to dance between our ears but never beyond when we were still using.

Aaron Z.

אִלּוּ הוֹצִיאָנוּ מִמִּצְרַיִם
וְלֹא עָשָׂה בָהֶם שְׁפָטִים,
דַּיֵּנוּ.

אִלּוּ עָשָׂה בָהֶם שְׁפָטִים,
וְלֹא עָשָׂה בֵאלֹהֵיהֶם,
דַּיֵּנוּ.

A Reading in Honor of Jerusalem Reunification Day
YOM YERUSHALAYIM - 28 Iyar - June 1-2, 2000

Israel fills us with pride. Many of us can recall when there was neither a flag to hoist nor a land to claim as our own. For others, Israel has been a living, breathing reality, for we have grown up as she has. At this time, all of us reflect on the meaning of Israel in our lives:

For the ingathering of our people from all corners of the world, **Dayeinu**

For the rebuilding of the Jewish homeland and reclaiming the land of Eretz Yisrael, **Dayeinu**

For absorbing the survivors of the Holocaust, **Dayeinu**

For the strength and security Israel provides to Jews in need, **Dayeinu**

For integrating the Jews from Europe, Africa, Asia, America, Ashkenazim and Sefaradim, **Dayeinu**

For the rejuvenation of art and poetry, music and dance, drama and literature, **Dayeinu**

For the growth of Jewish wisdom and knowledge, enlightening all of us in God's ways, **Dayeinu**

For creating hope for peace anew and illuminating the vision of a better world, **Dayeinu**

For enabling Torah once more to go forth from the Land of Zion and the word of God from Jerusalem, **Dayeinu**

Prepared by United Jewish Communities Rabbinic Cabinet

**If He had brought us out from Egypt,
and had not carried out judgments against them
Dayenu, it would have sufficed us!**

**If He had carried out judgments against them,
and not against their idols
Dayenu, it would have sufficed us!**

אִלּוּ עָשָׂה בֵאלֹהֵיהֶם,
וְלֹא הָרַג אֶת בְּכוֹרֵיהֶם,
דַּיֵּנוּ.

אִלּוּ הָרַג אֶת בְּכוֹרֵיהֶם
וְלֹא נָתַן לָנוּ אֶת מָמוֹנָם,
דַּיֵּנוּ.

אִלּוּ נָתַן לָנוּ אֶת מָמוֹנָם
וְלֹא קָרַע לָנוּ אֶת הַיָּם,
דַּיֵּנוּ.

אִלּוּ קָרַע לָנוּ אֶת הַיָּם
וְלֹא הֶעֱבִירָנוּ בְתוֹכוֹ בֶּחָרָבָה,
דַּיֵּנוּ.

אִלּוּ הֶעֱבִירָנוּ בְתוֹכוֹ בֶּחָרָבָה
וְלֹא שִׁקַּע צָרֵנוּ בְּתוֹכוֹ,
דַּיֵּנוּ.

אִלּוּ שִׁקַּע צָרֵנוּ בְּתוֹכוֹ
וְלֹא סִפֵּק צָרְכֵּנוּ בַּמִּדְבָּר אַרְבָּעִים שָׁנָה,
דַּיֵּנוּ.

אִלּוּ סִפֵּק צָרְכֵּנוּ בַּמִּדְבָּר אַרְבָּעִים שָׁנָה
ולֹא הֶאֱכִילָנוּ אֶת הַמָּן,
דַּיֵּנוּ.

If He had destroyed their idols,
and had not smitten their first-born
Dayenu, it would have sufficed us!

If He had smitten their first-born,
and had not given us their wealth
Dayenu, it would have sufficed us!

If He had given us their wealth,
and had not split the sea for us
Dayenu, it would have sufficed us!

If He had split the sea for us,
and had not taken us through it on dry land
Dayenu, it would have sufficed us!

If He had taken us through the sea on dry land, and had not drowned our oppressors in it **Dayenu, it would have sufficed us!**

If He had drowned our oppressors in it, and had not supplied our needs in the desert for forty years **Dayenu, it would have sufficed us!**

If He had supplied our needs in the desert for forty years, and had not fed us the manna
Dayenu, it would have sufficed us!

אִלּוּ הֶאֱכִילָנוּ אֶת הַמָּן
וְלֹא נָתַן לָנוּ אֶת הַשַּׁבָּת,
דַּיֵּנוּ.

אִלּוּ נָתַן לָנוּ אֶת הַשַּׁבָּת,
וְלֹא קֵרְבָנוּ לִפְנֵי הַר סִינַי,
דַּיֵּנוּ.

אִלּוּ קֵרְבָנוּ לִפְנֵי הַר סִינַי,
וְלֹא נָתַן לָנוּ אֶת הַתּוֹרָה,
דַּיֵּנוּ.

אִלּוּ נָתַן לָנוּ אֶת הַתּוֹרָה
וְלֹא הִכְנִיסָנוּ לְאֶרֶץ יִשְׂרָאֵל,
דַּיֵּנוּ.

אִלּוּ הִכְנִיסָנוּ לְאֶרֶץ יִשְׂרָאֵל
וְלֹא בָּנָה לָנוּ אֶת בֵּית הַבְּחִירָה,
דַּיֵּנוּ.

Connecting to Community

The transition to a nation based around the individual Jewish community came about in the aftermath of the destruction of the Second Temple in 70 C.E. With the destruction of all the symbols of its former sovereignty, largely based around the Temple and the cluster of institutions associated with it, there was a need to reorganize the Jewish people in a

If He had fed us the manna, and had not given us the Shabbat **Dayenu, it would have sufficed us!**

If He had given us the Shabbat, and had not brought us before Mount Sinai **Dayenu, it would have sufficed us!**

If He had brought us before Mount Sinai, and had not given us the Torah **Dayenu, it would have sufficed us!**

If He had given us the Torah, and had not brought us into the land of Israel **Dayenu, it would have sufficed us!**

If He had brought us into the land of Israel, and had not built for us the Beit Hamikdash **Dayenu, it would have sufficed us!**

....

new manner. If this had not occurred, it is difficult to see how the Jews could have survived as a collective, with the center of the nation ripped out of the national fabric. The people who provided the rescue plan, allowing the nation to move forward, were the group of scholars based at Yavneh, under the leadership of Rabbi Yochanan ben Zakkai and, later on, Rabbi Gamaliel.

It is difficult to overstate the importance of community in the Jewish story. All nations and peoples sub-divide into individual geographical communities that form the substructure underpinning the national framework. However, the peculiarity of the Jews as a people who have spent most of their history in Diaspora has caused the community to become a substitute for the nation. That is, many generations of Jews throughout

Dayenu

"Dayenu" is a very simple, yet beautiful poem – containing fifteen stanzas describing acts of God's kindness – each stanza stating that it would have been "enough" had God only helped us in one way.

However, some of those statements appear very strange, for they include that it "would have been enough had we not received the Torah", which simply doesn't make sense!

To understand what we are "really saying" in "dayneu", we must consider its context, as well as it content.

Within this context, the refrain of "dayenu" has an implicit suffix. In other words, "dayenu" should not be translated simply as "it would have been enough"; rather, "dayenu" means **"it would have been enough – to PRAISE God,** i.e. to say Hallel – even if God had only taken us out of Egypt, or only if He had split the Sea, etc.

In this manner, the poem poetically summarizes each significant stage of redemption, from the time of the Exodus until Am Yisrael's conquest of the Land – stating that each single act of God's kindness in that process obligates us to praise Him. For example:

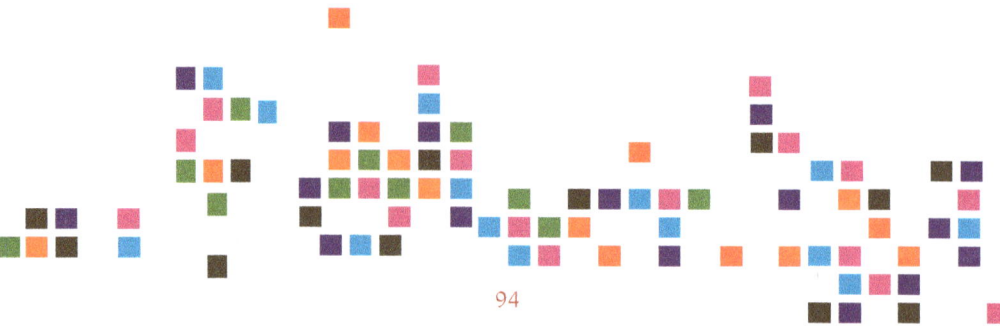

history have experienced their nationhood through life in their specific Jewish community. In the absence of national structures, the community not only replaced the nation; to a large extent, it became the nation.

Steve Israel

Had He only taken us out of Egypt and not punished the Egyptians, **it would have been reason enough** to say Hallel – Had He split the sea, but not given us the "manna", that alone **would have been reason enough** to say Hallel... And so on.

"Dayenu" is toward the concluding Maggid – or historical-section of the Haggadah and it sets the stage for Hallel, as we will now praise God.

It is the understanding and appreciation of each step of the redemptive process, which "dayenu" can teach us. "Ge'ulat Yisra'el" – the redemption of Israel – even in our time, is a process which is comprised of many stages. Every significant step in this process, freedom to study Torah, bringing us to the land of Israel, victory in battle in ancient times or contemporary, partial borders or the modern State of Israel, even without complete redemption, requires our gratitude and praise to Hashem.

For each stage in that process, it is incumbent upon Am Yisrael to recognize that stage and thank Hashem accordingly, while at the same time recognizing that many more stages remain yet unfulfilled – and reminding ourselves of how we need act -to be deserving of that next stage.

Rabbi Menachem Leibtag

עַל אַחַת, כַּמָּה וְכַמָּה, טוֹבָה כְפוּלָה וּמְכֻפֶּלֶת לַמָּקוֹם עָלֵינוּ:

שֶׁהוֹצִיאָנוּ מִמִּצְרַיִם, וְעָשָׂה בָהֶם שְׁפָטִים, וְעָשָׂה בֵאלֹהֵיהֶם, וְהָרַג אֶת בְּכוֹרֵיהֶם, וְנָתַן לָנוּ אֶת מָמוֹנָם, וְקָרַע לָנוּ אֶת הַיָּם, וְהֶעֱבִירָנוּ בְתוֹכוֹ בֶּחָרָבָה, וְשִׁקַּע צָרֵינוּ בְּתוֹכוֹ, וְסִפֵּק צָרְכֵּנוּ בַּמִּדְבָּר אַרְבָּעִים שָׁנָה, וְהֶאֱכִילָנוּ אֶת הַמָּן, וְנָתַן לָנוּ אֶת הַשַּׁבָּת, וְקֵרְבָנוּ לִפְנֵי הַר סִינַי, וְנָתַן לָנוּ אֶת הַתּוֹרָה, וְהִכְנִיסָנוּ לְאֶרֶץ יִשְׂרָאֵל, וּבָנָה לָנוּ אֶת בֵּית הַבְּחִירָה לְכַפֵּר עַל כָּל עֲוֹנוֹתֵינוּ.

Approach #3
We Are Still Servants to a Physical World

"And the Tablets are the handiwork of G-d, and the handwriting is the handwriting of G-d *charus* (engraved) on the Tablets." Do not read "*charus*" (engraved) but "*cheirus*" (freedom), for you have no free man except the one engaged in the study of Torah. (*Pirkei Avos 6:2*)

I have often pondered the meaning of this cryptic teaching. The study of Torah makes one free? The one and only path to freedom? I understand that the Torah makes life more meaningful, more spiritual, more enjoyable, more truthful…but more free?

The Maharal explains that the concept of slavery can refer only to the physical body. The body, interfacing with the physical world, is enslaved by the laws of the universe. The spiritual world, on the other hand, is not enslaved by these laws, since it is a world of "form" and not one of "matter."

Thus how much more so should we be grateful to the Omnipresent for the doubled and redoubled goodness that He has bestowed upon us;

for He has brought us out of Egypt, and carried out judgments against them, and against their idols, and smote their first-born, and gave us their wealth, and split the sea for us, and took us through it on dry land, and drowned our oppressors in it, and supplied our needs in the desert for forty years, and fed us the manna, and gave us the Shabbat, and brought us before Mount Sinai, and gave us the Torah, and brought us into the land of Israel and built for us the Beit Habechirah to atone for all our sins.

....

> According to Pirkei Avos, Torah study is not merely one avenue to freedom; rather, it is the only avenue to freedom. Even an absolute monarch of a vast domain with abundant wealth and prodigious power is not free, as he always faces the threat of the insurrection of his subjects. Only one involved in the spiritual, the eternal, is capable of transcending the physical world absolutely, and dominating absolutely the physical universe.

> Torah study is obviously more than casual perusal; to achieve the freedom of the Torah, it must be "engraved on the tablets of our heart;" it must be lived.
>
> By elevating the physical and infusing it with the "form" of Torah and mitzvahs, the Torah scholar transcends the limitations of the material world; he frees himself from the deterioration and decay of the physical by converting finite physical matter into infinite spiritual form. He is truly free.
>
> "Let freedom reign" in the Jewish heart! Only then is there a chance for the Jewish people to be "a light unto the nations," and for the nations of the world to recognize that since true freedom is possible, they no longer need to "escape from freedom!"
>
> Rabbi Pinchas Kantrowitz

רַבָּן גַּמְלִיאֵל הָיָה אוֹמֵר: כָּל שֶׁלֹּא אָמַר שְׁלֹשָׁה דְּבָרִים אֵלּוּ בַּפֶּסַח, לֹא יָצָא יְדֵי חוֹבָתוֹ, וְאֵלּוּ הֵן:

פֶּסַח, מַצָּה, וּמָרוֹר.

Achdut – Jewish Unity

One of these matters – which has possibly been the "hottest" topic of the past few years – is Unity. Everyone, both in and outside of Israel, writes and speaks about the problems of Israeli society, its internal differences and rifts.

Not all the fights that occur here are about vain things. It must be remembered that some of the issues about which we argue and fight are indeed serious and painful ones, and it would be wrong to state that none of the differences of opinion is of any importance.

> ### The Hidden Hand That Had Given
>
> We have been recipients of the choicest bounties of heaven. We have been preserved, these many years, in peace and prosperity... But we have forgotten God. We have forgotten the gracious hand which preserved us in peace, and multiplied and enriched and strengthened us; and we have vainly imagined, in the deceitfulness of our hearts, that all these blessings were produced by some superior wisdom and virtue of our own.
>
> Abraham Lincoln

Rabban Gamliel used to say: Whoever does not discuss the following three things on Passover has not fulfilled his duty, namely:

Passover (the Passover-sacrifice),
Matzah (the unleavened bread)
and Maror (the bitter herbs).

- - -

> Yet however unpleasant, or even dangerous, this may be, it is still within the norm. Quite often, though, our internal fighting slides toward a point which I find both dangerous and frightening. I am not making this up. I have seen such statements in newspapers, and even heard them from individuals - some of them people who are not considered extremists - from all walks of Jewish society. Everyone – those with the earlocks and those who go bare-headed, women with kerchiefs and women whose garments reveal more than they hide – speak in exactly the same manner about the "others." They say, "What have I got to do with them? We have nothing in common." I have heard people make statements such as, "Nothing in the

world ties me to those religious people; I feel much closer to the Arabs" - along with parallel statements from the other side: "Those secularists, they are just like the gentiles." Similarly, "settlers" and "left-wingers" may consider each other total strangers.

Such statements are already beyond fighting. They express some kind of acceptance, but a very threatening one: it is acceptance of the same kind that comes after death. I cease to fight because there is no one to fight with anymore. The other party has changed, has become a stranger. Seeing the other not as an enemy, an opponent to be fought against, but rather as a stranger, seems to me the greatest, most terrible threat to our existence. So long as I assume that I am right and the other party is wrong, we are still in one group, we still belong to the same body. I can say that so-and-so is a wicked person and an unbeliever, and should be put to death in all the four forms of capital punishment - and still feel that a non-believer is closer to me than a righteous gentile. Losing the feeling that we are one, that we are one body, is graver than any controversy, even more than a civil war.

A simile can help us understand this. Diseases of the auto-immune system have become more and more widespread nowadays. The basic point about these diseases, which is also their mystery, is that cells begin to treat certain parts of the body as foreign bodies. Every living organism has something that defines it; the body knows itself. When a part of the body is hurt or wounded, the body always feels: this is I, whatever is now causing me pain is me. In the auto-immune diseases, the "I" ceases to identify itself; the picture of the "I" becomes partial, stilted, reduced. And

מַרְאֶה בַּיָד עַל הַזְרוֹעַ וְיִזָהֵר שֶׁלֹא לְהַגְבִּיהַ אוֹתָה.

פֶּסַח שֶׁהָיוּ אֲבוֹתֵינוּ אוֹכְלִים בִּזְמַן שֶׁבֵּית הַמִּקְדָשׁ הָיָה קַיָם, עַל שׁוּם מָה?
עַל שׁוּם שֶׁפָּסַח הַקָדוֹשׁ בָּרוּךְ הוּא עַל בָּתֵי אֲבוֹתֵינוּ בְּמִצְרַיִם, שֶׁנֶאֱמַר: "וַאֲמַרְתֶּם: זֶבַח פֶּסַח הוּא לַיי, אֲשֶׁר פָּסַח עַל בָּתֵּי בְּנֵי יִשְׂרָאֵל בְּמִצְרַיִם בְּנָגְפּוֹ אֶת מִצְרַיִם, וְאֶת בָּתֵינוּ הִצִיל, וַיִקֹד הָעָם וַיִשְׁתַחֲווּ". (שמות י"ב כ"ז)

then, some of the cells begin to do what they would do against any foreign body: they try to eject it. They become incapable of perceiving the former complex "I."

So long as the Jewish "I" knows that a Jew is a Jew - however much he may fight with him or be willing to cast him to hell - that is a different, much more intimate and personal case; it is my own self, a part of my "I."

When we examine the referent - the state of the Jewish nation - we see that this simile has both theoretical and practical implications. It is not just a statement made on the spiritual, ideological level: it also has practical conclusions. I am not talking about creating unity. Unity is a grandiose thing, a supreme cause, and God willing, the time will come in which we shall attain it. I am talking about something closer, which is also more essential: pulling out of the syndrome of this incurable disease, in which I cease to feel my "I," which includes the other as well. I may have a very negative view of the Reform, Conservative and Reconstructionists - but still, they are I. So long as this joint "I" exists, we have life. It is this all-inclusive "I" of the Jewish people - not a unified Jewish people, but a people that has an "I" of its own, that includes all its members - that we must not lose.

Rabbi Adin Steinsaltz

Point to the shank-bone on the Seder Plate and without lifting it up, say:

The Passover-lamb that our fathers ate during the time of the Beit Hamikdash, for what reason? Because the Omnipresent passed over our fathers' houses in Egypt, as it is said: "You shall say, It is a Passover-offering to Hashem, because He passed over the houses of the children of Israel in Egypt when He struck the Egyptians with a plague, and He saved our houses. And the people bowed and prostrated themselves." (Exodus 12:27)

The Value of Appreciation

Most societies value the expression of appreciation and recognize its ability to smooth the rough edges of interpersonal relations. For this reason, we make a point of teaching our children to express thanks from a very early age. We strive to instill gratitude as a habit, even if at times we know the feeling behind the gesture may be lacking. We sense intuitively that a society which devalues or denigrates the concept of gratitude – that defines relationships by functionality alone – cannot, and probably ought not to, thrive... The structure of giving thanks on a regular basis, even in hard times, encourages us to focus on the positive side of life. It does not mean that we forget the dark side, just that we keep a true perspective, giving the positive side its due... In the end, feeling and expressing gratitude is good for us. The Almighty does not "need" our thanksgiving. It is we who benefit from feeling and expressing it.

                        Rabbi Adin Steinsaltz

Internal Transformation – Searching for Chametz Within

"Of all the commandments associated with Pesach, there is one that, due to the severity of its transgression, stands out from all the others. On Pesach, one is not permitted to have in one's possession any "Chametz," leaven substances. One can not eat or own bread or any product that is leaven during Pesach. The only "flour" product permitted is Matzot, a cracker–like bread made from a dough consisting of only flour and water, which is not allowed to rise. In order to assure that our homes are Chametz – free for Pesach, we go through extensive cleaning and preparing, to assure that not even a crumb of Chametz will be found or seen during Pesach.

Our Sages have told us that Chametz and the preparations associated with it are extremely symbolic. Chametz represents the evil within us, our Yetzer HoRa – our Evil Inclination. It represents all of our character flaws such as haughtiness, jealousy, unbridled passion and lust. Just as we need to remove every speck of Chametz from our household, so too we need to remove every speck of spiritual Chametz from our beings. Just as much time and effort is expended on preparing ourselves physically for Pesach, by removing any hint of Chametz, we must also exert much time and effort on preparing ourselves spiritually for Pesach, by working on improving our character, which is accomplished by removing all the evil traits we unfortunately carry with us.

Every Jewish holiday has a general theme or objective. Every holiday is designed to be transformative. In Yom Kippur the objective is to personally reflect on what went wrong and how we might do better. On Channuka the objective is to remember the historical military and provendential guidance of the past to influence us today. On Shavuos the goal is to reflect on the nature of the revelation of the Torah and to reaccept its principals and requirements. The list can continue and every Jewish holiday is designed to change us, to recharge and remind us and to motivate us to be better toward our fellow man, better toward our relationship with God and better with our relationship with ourselves. Pesach is no exception to the goals of transformation.

Rabbi Yehudah Prero

עוֹרֵךְ הַסֵּדֶר מַגְבִּיהַּ אֶת הַמַּצּוֹת, מַרְאֶה אוֹתָן לַמְסֻבִּים וְאוֹמֵר:

מַצָּה זוֹ שֶׁאָנוּ אוֹכְלִים, עַל שׁוּם מָה?

עַל שׁוּם שֶׁלֹּא הִסְפִּיק בְּצֵקָם שֶׁל אֲבוֹתֵינוּ לְהַחֲמִיץ עַד שֶׁנִּגְלָה עֲלֵיהֶם מֶלֶךְ מַלְכֵי הַמְּלָכִים, הַקָּדוֹשׁ בָּרוּךְ הוּא, וּגְאָלָם, שֶׁנֶּאֱמַר: "וַיֹּאפוּ אֶת הַבָּצֵק אֲשֶׁר הוֹצִיאוּ מִמִּצְרַיִם עֻגֹת מַצּוֹת, כִּי לֹא חָמֵץ, כִּי גֹרְשׁוּ מִמִּצְרַיִם וְלֹא יָכְלוּ לְהִתְמַהְמֵהַּ, וְגַם צֵדָה לֹא עָשׂוּ לָהֶם". (שמות י"ב ל"ט)

The Stories of Six Survivors Who Have Rebuilt Their Lives in Israel

Menachem Katz was born in 1925 in Berezhany, Poland, to a religious Zionist family. In 1941, the Germans occupied Berezhany, and Ukrainians and Germans murdered many Jews. In October 1942, the town's ghetto was established, and on Yom Kippur of 1942, hundreds of Jews were deported. Together with 30 other people, Katz's family hid in a secret room in the ghetto and thus escaped deportation.

In the spring of 1943, the Nazis established a labor camp near the ghetto, where Katz and his stepfather Eliyahu were taken to work. Two weeks later, the ghetto was liquidated. Eliyahu committed suicide.

Katz hid with his mother and younger sister at the home of a Polish farmer, Pyotr Kameitz. Kameitz, his wife Henka and their two daughters

---

מַגְבִּיהַּ אֶת הַמָּרוֹר לַמְסֻבִּים וּמַרְאֶה אוֹתוֹ לַמְסֻבִּים וְאוֹמֵר:

מָרוֹר זֶה שֶׁאָנוּ אוֹכְלִים, עַל שׁוּם מָה?

Take the broken Matzah into your hand and say:

This Matzah that we eat for what reason? Because the dough of our fathers did not have time to become leavened before the King of the kings of kings, the Holy One, blessed be He, revealed Himself to them and redeemed them. Thus it is said: "They baked Matzah-cakes from the dough that they had brought out of Egypt, because it was not leavened; for they had been driven out of Egypt and could not delay, and they had also not prepared any [other] provisions." (Exodus 12:29)

. . . .

---

were later recognized by Yad Vashem as Righteous Among the Nations. In the spring of 1944, the family fled into the forest, where they remained until the liberation of Berezhany in July 1944.

In October 1946, Katz, his mother and his sister Rina sailed for Israel. Katz studied architecture at the Technion in Haifa. He won many prizes in his field, published a book on architecture and designed the museum at Kibbutz Baram in memory of the Jews of Berezhany. He is currently working on restoring the Berezhany synagogue.

Jpost.com, April 29 2008

Lift the maror from the Seder Plate and show to the Seder participants and say:

This maror that we eat for what reason?

עַל שׁוּם שֶׁמֵּרְרוּ הַמִּצְרִים אֶת חַיֵּי אֲבוֹתֵינוּ בְּמִצְרַיִם, שֶׁנֶּאֱמַר: "וַיְמָרְרוּ אֶת חַיֵּיהֶם בַּעֲבֹדָה קָשָׁה, בְּחֹמֶר וּבִלְבֵנִים וּבְכָל עֲבֹדָה בַּשָּׂדֶה אֵת כָּל עֲבֹדָתָם אֲשֶׁר עָבְדוּ בָהֶם בְּפָרֶךְ". (שמות א' י"ד)

בְּכָל דּוֹר וָדוֹר חַיָּב אָדָם לִרְאוֹת אֶת עַצְמוֹ כְּאִלּוּ הוּא יָצָא מִמִּצְרַיִם,

שֶׁנֶּאֱמַר: "וְהִגַּדְתָּ לְבִנְךָ בַּיּוֹם הַהוּא לֵאמֹר, בַּעֲבוּר זֶה עָשָׂה יְיָ לִי בְּצֵאתִי מִמִּצְרָיִם". (שמות י"ג ח')
לֹא אֶת אֲבוֹתֵינוּ בִּלְבַד גָּאַל הַקָּדוֹשׁ בָּרוּךְ הוּא, אֶלָּא אַף אוֹתָנוּ גָּאַל עִמָּהֶם, שֶׁנֶּאֱמַר: "וְאוֹתָנוּ הוֹצִיא מִשָּׁם, לְמַעַן הָבִיא אֹתָנוּ, לָתֶת לָנוּ אֶת הָאָרֶץ אֲשֶׁר נִשְׁבַּע לַאֲבֹתֵינוּ".
(דברים ו' כ"ג)

Concepts in Freedom - Approach #4:
Freedom to Conceive Intellectually

The intellectual process of posing questions concerning the accepted order while comparing it to other orders, existent or imaginary, is the very essence of human freedom. The difference between slaves, whose minds are subjugated, and free people in an open society, is the ability to

Because the Egyptians embittered our fathers' lives in Egypt, as it is said: "They made their lives bitter with hard service, with mortar and with bricks, and with all manner of service in the field; all their service which they made them serve with rigor." (Exodus 1, 14)

In every generation a person is obligated to regard himself as if he had come out of Egypt,

as it is said: "You shall tell your child on that day, it is because of this that Hashem did for me when I left Egypt." (Exodus 13:8) The Holy One, blessed be He, redeemed not only our fathers from Egypt, but He redeemed also us with them, as it is said: "It was us that He brought out from there, so that He might bring us to give us the land that He swore to our fathers." (Deuteronomy 6:23)

---

conceive of a different life, a different social order.

Slaves rebel against their masters not because of their urge for freedom of expression, but rather because they have discovered another possible world order in which they need not live as slaves.

Slaves born into slavery may imagine that it is their nature to be subjugated and the tyrannical social order into which they have been born reflects the natural order, or the divine order. Moses, however, who was born into slavery but who grew up in Pharoah's palace, is able to comprehend both humiliation and the meaning of freedom.

"Perhaps, Moshe had to grow up in the King's palace so his soul would become accustomed to a higher level, not a degraded one, like the slaves who have become habituated to the House of Bondage" [and who will not rise up against injustice and who do not feel the indignity of a lack of freedom]. (Quoting Nechama Leibowitz)

Similarly, it was Theodor Herzl, the assimilated Jew who grew up in a Western society during the onset of democracy and the rise of German nationalism who was able to become the visionary of the Jewish state, bringing to his brethren in autocratic Eastern Europe, the vision of liberal national freedom.

Questioning is related to the tendency of Jews throughout the Diaspora to be original in whatever they do. This phenomenon is called in sociological terminology, the "creativity of the marginal man."

Noam Zion

Gratitude Should Be Long Lasting

Let your gratitude to others last for a long time. A classic American joke tells of a congressman who, when he solicits a constituent's vote, learns that the man is planning to vote for his opponent. "But how can you do that?" the congressman objects. "Don't you remember that time ten years ago when your business burned down, and I arranged for you to a low-interest loan from the Small Business Administration? And what about the time when your daughter got in trouble with the police overseas, and I arranged for her to be released and sent back to the United States? And the time when your wife was sick, and I helped get her admitted to the special hospital she needed?" The voter answers, "That's all true, but what have you done for me lately?"

Rabbi Joseph Telushkin

The Carrot, the Egg, and the Coffee Bean

A young woman went to her mother and told her about her life and how things were so hard for her. She did not know how she was going to make it and wanted to give up. She was tired of fighting and struggling.

It seemed that, as one problem was solved, a new one arose. Her mother took her to the kitchen. She filled three pots with water and placed each on a high fire. Soon the pots came to a boil. In the first, she placed carrots, in the second she placed eggs, and in the last she placed ground coffee beans.

She let them sit and boil, without saying a word. In about twenty minutes, she turned off the burners. She fished the carrots out and placed them in a bowl. She pulled the eggs out and placed them in a bowl. Then she ladled the coffee out and placed it in a bowl. Turning to her daughter, she asked, "Tell me, what do you see?"

"Carrots, eggs, and coffee," the young woman replied. The mother brought her closer and asked her to feel the carrots. She did and noted that they were soft. She then asked her to take an egg and break it. After pulling off the shell, she observed the hard-boiled egg. Finally, she asked her to sip the coffee. The daughter smiled as she tasted its rich aroma. The daughter then asked, "What does it mean, mother?"

Her mother explained that each of these objects had faced the same adversity – boiling water – but each reacted differently. The carrot went in strong, hard and unrelenting. However, after being subjected to the boiling water, it softened and became weak.

The egg had been fragile. Its thin outer shell had protected its liquid interior. But, after sitting through the boiling water, its inside became hardened! The ground coffee beans were unique, however.

After they were in the boiling water, they had changed the water.

"Which are you?" the mother asked her daughter. "When adversity knocks on your door, how do you respond? Are you a carrot, an egg, or a coffee bean?" Think of this: Which am I? Am I the carrot that seems strong but, with pain and adversity, do I wilt and become soft and lose my strength? Am I the egg that starts with a malleable heart, but changes with the heat? Did I have a fluid spirit but, after a death, a breakup, or a financial hardship, does my shell look the same, but on the inside am I bitter and tough with a stiff spirit and a hardened heart? Or am I like the coffee bean?

The bean actually changes the hot water, the very circumstance that brings the pain. When the water gets hot, it releases the fragrance and flavor.

If you are like the bean, when things are at their worst, you get better and change the situation around you. When the hours are the darkest and trials are their greatest, do you elevate to another level? How do you handle adversity? Are you a carrot, an egg, or a coffee bean?

Anonymous

Slavery Around Us

The Winter of 5605 [1945] was a difficult one in the Feihingen concentration camp in Germany. We suffered from arduous labor in the stone quarries, cold, and hunger; as well as an epidemic of typhus which killed many. To those who died of typhus were added the victims of the cruel murders of the SS men. The result was despair and apathy and indifference to our fate.

But in this death camp there were some who stubbornly held fast to their Judaism until the last moment. Passover was coming. How does one refrain from eating hametz? A few days before Pesah one of the SS men entered the foundry where I was working as a sign-maker. He asked if I could prepare some targets for rifle practice. At the moment an idea sprung into my mind and I proposed it to him I would prepare targets with figures of soldiers affixed to them. But I would need a quantity of flour with which to prepare the paste... ultimately I received fifteen kilos of flour. When I got the flour to the foundry I told my friends of the miracle – and it is impossible to describe their joy. The will to live, which was almost extinguished, was kindled anew. We "liberated" some wood, scraped a table with glass, and "kashered" it with hot bricks... we began to bake the matzot... On the night of the first seder we gathered in the foundry as the marranos did in ancient Spain. We started awesomely. "We were slaves." Each of us had three matzot. In place of wine we used water sweetened with sugar. We had potatoes for karpas, and white beets for maror. Salt and water were not in short supply. We recited the Haggadah from some siddurim which we had succeeded in hiding all this time. When we were about halfway through the Haggadah, Azriel began to preach to us not to despair and to withstand the test of affliction, for redemption was near...

Mordekhai Eliav

Long Road to Israel

We are duty-bound to envision ourselves as if we personally left Egypt. We, along with our family and friends, have endured great sorrow and hardships as slaves under Pharaoh's rule, and now, thanks to a series of miraculous plagues and political turmoil in our host country, we are making our way on foot to a land long ago promised.

Some of our closest relatives and friends perished during their servitude in Egypt. Some have elected to stay behind rather than face the uncertainties that lay ahead. We are armed and military conflict is certain. We have obtained arms from our former masters and anticipate defending ourselves should the Egyptians pursue us or should we encounter hostile enemies ahead of us. We might be weary due to our enslavement, but nonetheless we are strengthened by the desire to establish a home in peace in Israel.

This strong determination and sacrifice, in the face of fatigue, is poignantly expressed in *Self-Portrait of a Hero: The letters of Jonathan Netanyahu*. On 8/17/68, Netanyahu wrote the following to his parents:

> A kind of sadness has overtaken me, which doesn't leave me. It does not control me or direct my actions, but it is inside me, it exists, sunk in a well-hidden corner of my being. This isn't exactly an emptiness, but something with a very heavy deposit - a sort of "heavy emptiness." Perhaps this feeling doesn't exist only in me. There are times when I sense the cry and depth of this sadness in others, in all of those friends who came through the war with their bodies intact. I think we all came out of it wounded, changed, more sensitive, more caring, and much much older. That harmony that characterizes a young man's world is not part of me any more. Although I'm still young, still strong and confident of myself and my ability, I cannot ignore the fact that a sense of old age has taken hold of me... an old age particular to young men... not only the war, the killing, the deaths, the wounds and disabilities are to blame-- these can be overcome. Their imprint may perhaps be dulled by time. The real cause is the sense of helplessness in the face of a war that has no end... It continues with every mine and killing and murder... I have no doubt that war will come. Nor do I doubt that we will win. But for how long? Until when? We can't wipe out the Arab people; they are too many and have too much support. Of course we shall go on striking them, again and again and again, and we shall be fully justified in delivering a more powerful blow each time. Knowing this makes us feel good, but the good feeling is mixed with sadness. We're young and we were not born for wars alone. I intend to go on with my studies...

Jonathan Netanyahu was killed rescuing Jewish captives in the raid on Entebbe.

Passover Transcends Generations

In more ways than one, Passover is the much sought-after fountain of youth. One never outgrows one's identity as a child in relation to Passover. According to *halacha*, even if one is old and totally alone, he must begin the Seder with asking the four questions. Asking of whom? Why, God of course! We are never without a father. If one is not in the company of children, one becomes the child oneself.

The *Haggadah* states, "In every generation, a person must view oneself

מְכַסִּים אֶת הַמָּצוֹת, מַגְבִּיהִים אֶת הכוס עַד הַלְלוּיָהּ:

לְפִיכָךְ אֲנַחְנוּ חַיָּבִים לְהוֹדוֹת, לְהַלֵּל, לְשַׁבֵּחַ, לְפָאֵר, לְרוֹמֵם, לְהַדֵּר, לְבָרֵךְ, לְעַלֵּה וּלְקַלֵּס לְמִי שֶׁעָשָׂה לַאֲבוֹתֵינוּ וְלָנוּ אֶת כָּל הַנִּסִּים הָאֵלּוּ: הוֹצִיאָנוּ מֵעַבְדוּת לְחֵרוּת מִיָּגוֹן לְשִׂמְחָה, וּמֵאֵבֶל לְיוֹם טוֹב, וּמֵאֲפֵלָה לְאוֹר גָּדוֹל, וּמִשִּׁעְבּוּד לִגְאֻלָּה; וְנֹאמַר לְפָנָיו שִׁירָה חֲדָשָׁה: הַלְלוּיָהּ.

Gratitude for the Past and Present

.... Lefikach, Therefore, when a given event has a positive outcome, and moreover this event is personally meaningful, it is natural for one to be grateful. When one discovers that the event is not isolated, but rather is a catalyst for even greater changes, the gratitude is even more profound.

We have just concluded a brief but powerful description of the Exodus from Egypt. The miracles that God bestowed on the Jewish people in Egypt culminated in the freedom march of a previously enslaved people, and prepared them for their rendezvous with their Creator and a revelational experience at Mount Sinai. These providential experiences warrant our praise and gratitude.

> as having personally participated in the Exodus from Egypt, emancipated from slavery." Just as the individual can recapture his childhood, so must the nation re-experience its infancy. Individually and collectively, Passover is rejuvenation.
>
> It is one of the ironies of life that as children we wish to be grownups, and when we finally do grow up, we wish we could be children again. Passover allows us to be both child and adult.
>
> **Rabbi Abraham Twersky**

Cover the matzah and raise the cup. The cup is to be held in the hand until the completion of the blessing, "Who Has Redeemed Us..."

Thus it is our duty to thank, to laud, to praise, to glorify, to exalt, to adore, to bless, to elevate and to honor the One who did all these miracles for our fathers and for us: He took us from slavery to freedom, from sorrow to joy, and from mourning to festivity, and from deep darkness to great light and from bondage to redemption. **Let us therefore recite before Him Halleluyah, Praise God!**

> The paragraph speaks not only of the wonders performed for our forefathers, but also for us. Lest we have trouble feeling grateful for an event that occurred several thousands of years ago, let us remember that each Jew that participates in the Seder today has descended from people who survived, escaped or had the fortune to be distant from the Holocaust in Europe. Let us not forget our good fortune.

Freedom: A Choice of a Certain Action

Is that theory true which would have us believe that man is no more than a product of many conditional and environmental factors – be they biological, psychological or sociological nature? Is man but an accidental product of these? Most important, do the prisoners' reactions to the singular world of the concentration camp prove that man cannot escape the influences of his surroudings? Does man have no choice of action in the face of such circumstances?

We can answer these questions from experience as well as on principle. The experiences of camp life show that man does have a choice of action. There were enough examples, often of a heroic nature, which proved that apathy could be overcome, irritability suppressed. Man can preserve a vestige of spiritual freedom, of independence of mind, even in such terrible conditions of psychic and physical stress.

We who lived in concentration camps can remember the men who walked through the huts comforting others, giving away their last piece of bread. They may have been few in number, but they offer sufficient proof that everything can be taken from a man but one thing: the last of the human freedoms – to choose one's attitude in any given set of circumstances, to choose one's own way.

And there were always choices to make. Every day, every hour, offered the opportunity to make a decision, a decision which determined whether you would or would not submit to those powers which threatened to rob you of your very self, your inner freedom: which determined whether

הַלְלוּיָהּ, הַלְלוּ עַבְדֵי יְיָ הַלְלוּ אֶת שֵׁם יְיָ.
יְהִי שֵׁם יְיָ מְבֹרָךְ מֵעַתָּה וְעַד עוֹלָם.
מִמִּזְרַח שֶׁמֶשׁ עַד מְבוֹאוֹ מְהֻלָּל שֵׁם יְיָ.
רָם עַל כָּל גּוֹיִם יְיָ עַל הַשָּׁמַיִם כְּבוֹדוֹ.
מִי כַּייָ אֱלֹהֵינוּ הַמַּגְבִּיהִי לָשָׁבֶת.
הַמַּשְׁפִּילִי לִרְאוֹת בַּשָּׁמַיִם וּבָאָרֶץ.
מְקִימִי מֵעָפָר דָּל מֵאַשְׁפֹּת יָרִים אֶבְיוֹן.

> or not you would become the plaything of circumstance, renouncing freedom and dignity to become molded into the form of the typical inmate.
>
> **Victor Frankl**
>
> **Victor Frankl was a psychologist who survived the Auschwitz death camp.**

Personal Redemption

Shlomo Rokeach of Belz said, There are three Jewish exiles: the exile of the Jewish People from the Land; the Jew in exile from his fellow Jew; and the person in exile from his own self. What the Zohar calls Teshuvah Elyona, translated as "the highest repentance", but more roughly approximated in English as "Ultimate reclaiming", is the process of returning from this last exile, to our true divine selves.

Rabbi Abraham Isaac Kook, the first Chief Rabbi of Israel says, "It is only through the great truth of return to self, that humanity and the nation and the world… will return to its Creator, to the light, and the light of life. This is the secret of the light of the Messiah."

Editor's note: Redemption, that is to be understood as transformation, can and should occur on three levels: national, communal and personal.

Halleluya, Praise God! Offer praise, you servants of Hashem; praise the Name of Hashem. May Hashem's Name be blessed from now and to all eternity. From the rising of the sun to its setting, Hashem's Name is praised. Hashem is high above all nations, His glory is over the heavens. Who is like Hashem, our God, who dwells on high yet looks down so low upon heaven and earth! He raises the poor from the dust, He lifts the needy from the dunghill, to seat them with nobles, with the nobles

לְהוֹשִׁיבִי עִם נְדִיבִים עִם נְדִיבֵי עַמּוֹ.
מוֹשִׁיבִי עֲקֶרֶת הַבַּיִת אֵם הַבָּנִים שְׂמֵחָה
הַלְלוּ יָהּ. (תהלים קי"ג)

Thanking God for Israel

How can we not thank the Almighty for all the kindness that He has showered upon us? First and foremost, the State of Israel serves as a safe haven for five million Jews. After the nightmare of the Holocaust, hundreds of thousands of Jewish refugees wandered around the globe, finding a home and refuge only in Israel. The State has contributed an incalculable amount to the restoration of Jewish pride after the devastating chillul Hashem (desecration of God's Name) caused by the Holocaust. Today, too, the State plays an enormous role in the Jewish identity of our brethren throughout the world. For so many of them, the emotional attachment to the State remains the final thread connecting them to the Jewish People and to the God of Israel.

I spoke earlier of Rav Kook's inability to come to terms with the establishment of a state that would not bring to fruition the ultimate destiny of redemption. This led him to claim that the impending State of Israel was to be the ideal State of the period of ge'ula (redemption). But don't all the critical functions fulfilled by the State of Israel (as listed above) justify its existence, even if it has not developed into the ideal community?

Unlike the Charedim, we will not undermine the importance or legitimacy of the State; but our love for our country must not blind us from criticizing its shortcomings. We remain very, very far from the ideal Jewish State, and we must therefore do whatever we can to bring about its realization. A more just society and stronger public values are necessary prerequisites for its actualization. If we want to hasten the ultimate redemption, we must work harder to ensure moral values on both the individual and communal levels. Closing the social gaps, concern for the vulnerable elements of society, fighting poverty, respectful treatment of the non-Jews in Israel – all these measures will bring us closer to the day

of His people. He restores the barren woman to the house, into a joyful mother of children.
Halleluyah – praise God. (Psalms 113)

---

for which we long. We hope and believe that our State will develop into the ideal Jewish State, "the foundation of the Divine Throne in the world, whose entire desire is that God shall be One and His Name shall be One."

Harav Yehuda Amital

Being Grateful Prior to a Loss

A grateful person doesn't express happiness for what he has only when he's lost it. Gratitude consists in acknowledging the good in your life while your still have it.

When Rabbi Irving Lehman was a child in the 1920s, he accompanied his mother to get a *bracha*, blessing from the Lubavitcher Rebbe, who was then visiting the United States (it is a long-standing Jewish tradition to solicit a blessing from a person regarded as holy). They stood in line for hours, and when they finally reached the Rebbe, he asked her, "How are your children?"

"Baruch Hashem" (Thank God), Rabbi Lehman's mother answered.
"And how is your parnassah (livelihood)?"
"Baruch Hashem".
"How is your family's health?"
"Baruch Hashem".
"So then what kind of bracha do you want me to give you?"
The rebbe asked.
She answered : "Zol nisht farshtert veren" (it should not be spoiled).

Such is the attitude of the pious, a sense of appreciation for what they have, instead of a focus on of what they are missing.

Rabbi Joseph Telushkin

בְּצֵאת יִשְׂרָאֵל מִמִּצְרָיִם, בֵּית יַעֲקֹב מֵעַם לֹעֵז.
הָיְתָה יְהוּדָה לְקָדְשׁוֹ יִשְׂרָאֵל מַמְשְׁלוֹתָיו.
הַיָּם רָאָה וַיָּנֹס הַיַּרְדֵּן יִסֹּב לְאָחוֹר.
הֶהָרִים רָקְדוּ כְאֵילִים גְּבָעוֹת כִּבְנֵי צֹאן.
מַה לְּךָ הַיָּם כִּי תָנוּס הַיַּרְדֵּן תִּסֹּב לְאָחוֹר.
הֶהָרִים תִּרְקְדוּ כְאֵילִים גְּבָעוֹת כִּבְנֵי צֹאן.
מִלִּפְנֵי אָדוֹן חוּלִי אָרֶץ מִלִּפְנֵי אֱלוֹהַּ יַעֲקֹב.
הַהֹפְכִי הַצּוּר אֲגַם מָיִם חַלָּמִישׁ לְמַעְיְנוֹ מָיִם.

(תהלים קי"ד)

Paradox of Freedom

It is widely believed in modern industrialized societies that to maximize the general welfare the state or economy needs to maximize freedom. It follows that to maximize freedom the state or economy needs to maximize choices which means more freedom which means more general welfare.

Examples of the multiplicity of choices: think about how many salad dressings or cereals are available in a common large supermarket. Multiple health-care options for a given disease are now common with the final decision on treatment alternatives left up to the patient. The portability of computers and phones make office work possible from almost any location at almost any time.

Consider for a moment that the modern explosion of freedom and choices may have new and unintended disadvantages. For example:

1. Paralysis. With so many choices it is oft times difficult to decide on any given choice. Important decisions can be postponed at a cost.

When Israel went out of Egypt, the House of Jacob from a people of a foreign language, Judah became His holy one, Israel His dominion. The sea saw and fled, the Jordan turned backward. The mountains skipped like rams, the hills like young sheep. What is with you, O sea, that you flee; Jordan, that you turn backward? Mountains, why do you skip like rams; hills, like a pool of water, the flint-stone into a spring of water. (Psalms 114)

---

2. Less satisfaction. It is easy to imagine that after making a selection from a long list of choices that you could have made a better choice. The more options the more regret.
3. Opportunity costs. This means that having the freedom to make a choice and having done so it comes at the cost of another worthwhile choice. Doing this while you could have been doing that.
4. Escalation of expectations. With so many choices one expects the very best experience. The greater the options the greater the expectations.
5. Self blame. With so many choices if there is a level of disappointment who is responsible? The chooser.

This explosion of freedom and choice around us may make us less happy and less satisfied.

Barry Schwartz

כוס שניה

מַגְבִּיהִים אֶת הַכּוֹס עַד גָּאַל יִשְׂרָאֵל.
כָּל אֶחָד יִקַּח אֶת כּוֹסוֹ בְּיָדוֹ, וְיֹאמַר:

בָּרוּךְ אַתָּה יְיָ אֱלֹהֵינוּ מֶלֶךְ הָעוֹלָם, אֲשֶׁר גְּאָלָנוּ וְגָאַל אֶת אֲבוֹתֵינוּ מִמִּצְרַיִם, וְהִגִּיעָנוּ לַלַּיְלָה הַזֶּה לֶאֱכָל בּוֹ מַצָּה וּמָרוֹר.

כֵּן, יְיָ אֱלֹהֵינוּ וֵאלֹהֵי אֲבוֹתֵינוּ, יַגִּיעֵנוּ לְמוֹעֲדִים וְלִרְגָלִים אֲחֵרִים הַבָּאִים לִקְרָאתֵנוּ לְשָׁלוֹם. שְׂמֵחִים בְּבִנְיַן עִירֶךָ וְשָׂשִׂים בַּעֲבוֹדָתֶךָ, וְנֹאכַל שָׁם מִן הַזְּבָחִים וּמִן הַפְּסָחִים
(במוצאי שבת אומרים: מִן הַפְּסָחִים וּמִן הַזְּבָחִים) אֲשֶׁר יַגִּיעַ דָּמָם עַל קִיר מִזְבַּחֲךָ לְרָצוֹן, וְנוֹדֶה לְךָ שִׁיר חָדָשׁ עַל גְּאֻלָּתֵנוּ וְעַל פְּדוּת נַפְשֵׁנוּ. **בָּרוּךְ אַתָּה יְיָ גָּאַל יִשְׂרָאֵל.**

Redemption in an Instant

Oskar Schindler (28 April 1908 – 9 October 1974) was a German industrialist credited with saving almost 1,200 Jews during the Holocaust by having them work in his enamelware and ammunitions factories located in what is now Poland and the Czech Republic.

No one really knows what Schindler's motives were. However, he was quoted as saying, "I knew the people who worked for me… When you know people, you have to behave toward them like human beings."

The Second Cup

Lift the cup until Ga'al Yisrael.
Each person should lift his cup.

Blessed are You, God, our God, King of the universe, **who has redeemed us and redeemed our fathers from Egypt, and enabled us to attain this night to eat matzah and maror.** So too, God, our God and God of our fathers, enable us to attain other holidays and festivals that will come to us in peace with happiness in the rebuilding of Your city, and with rejoicing in Your service [in the Bet Hamikdash]. Then we shall eat (Note: if the festival is on any day except Saturday night say: of the sacrifices and of the Passover-offerings; if the Seder is on Saturday Night say: of the Passover-offerings and of the sacrifices) whose blood shall be sprinkled on the wall of Your altar for acceptance; and we shall thank You with a new song for our redemption and for the deliverance of our souls. **Blessed are You, Hashem, who redeemed Israel.**

The following paragraph is excerpted from the biography of Oskar Schindler by Thomas Keneally and the dialogue is excerpted from the movie Schindler's List by Steven Spielberg:

> It became clear from announcements on the radio that the war was over and the exact time to end all hostility was declared. A meeting was held at the Schindler factory that included all the soon-to-be freed prisoners and all of their captors. The meeting was at night – the last night of the war in Europe – and was tense, solemn and quiet. Schindler eloquently called for a peaceful separation between the guards and when it was over, the SS left the hall quickly. The prisoners remained. They looked around and wondered if they were at last the possessors. As Oskar moved outside toward his apartment to pack, a group of prisoners intercepted him and presented him with a gold ring that was made the day before from gold donated from a prisoner's teeth and fashioned into a gift.

Oskar Schindler spent some time admiring the ring. All was quiet. All was still. He showed the inscription to Itzchak and asked for a translation.

Itzchak: It is from the Talmud. It reads, "He who saves a single life saves an entire world in time."

Oskar: From where is the gold?

Itzchak: It was given by Jereth - from his dental bridgework.

Oskar became very solemn and slowly placed the ring on his finger.

Oskar: I could have done more. (pauses) I could have done more.

Itzchak: There are eleven hundred people who are alive because of you. (gestures with his arm at the crowd around him)

Oskar: If I had made more money. I threw away so much money. You have no idea. If I just...

Itzchak: You have no humiliations because of what you did.

Oskar: I did not do enough.

Itzchak: You did so much.

Oskar: This car. (gestures toward his car) I could have sold this car. Why did I need this car? Ten people right there. Ten people! Ten more people. This pin: (removes a lapel pin from his suit coat) Two more people. It is gold. Two more people! Would have given me two for it. At least one. One more. One more person and I didn't. One more person and I didn't.

Unity Is Crucial When Facing an Adversary

At the end of the Goblet of Fire, Professor Dumbledore delivers some well-chosen words about the need for unity among students and all "wizardfolk" who oppose the evil wizard Voldemort:

> *Every guest in this hall ... will be welcomed back here, at any time, should they wish to come. I say to you all, once again -- in light of Voldemort's return, we are only as strong as we are united, as weak as we are divided.*
>
> *"Voldemort's gift for spreading discord and enmity is very great. We can only fight it by showing an equally strong bond of friendship and trust. Differences of habit and language are nothing at all if our aims are identical and our hearts are open.* (Goblets of Fire, chapter 37)

The next year, the sorting hat, the magical talking hat whose job it is to divide the students into the four schoolhouses, infuses the same theme into its start-of-year song:

> *"...And now the sorting hat is here*
> *And you all know the score:*
> *I sort you into houses*
> *Because that's what I'm for.*
> *But this year I'll go further,*
> *Listen closely to my song:*
> *Though condemned I am to split you*
> *Still I worry that it's wrong.*
> *...*
> *Oh, know the peril, read the signs,*
> *The warning history shows.*
> *For our Hogwarts is in danger*
> *From external deadly foes.*
> *And we must unite inside her*
> *Or we'll crumble from within.*
> *I have told you, I have warned you...*
> *Let the Sorting now begin."*

(Order of the Phoenix, chapter 11)

Dov Krulwich

שׁוֹתִין אֶת הַכּוֹס בַּהֲסָבַת שְׂמֹאל.

הִנְנִי מוּכָן וּמְזוּמָּן לְקַיֵּם מִצְוַת כּוֹס שְׁנִיָּה מֵאַרְבַּע כּוֹסוֹת.

בָּרוּךְ אַתָּה יְיָ אֱלֹהֵינוּ מֶלֶךְ הָעוֹלָם בּוֹרֵא פְּרִי הַגָּפֶן.

Today We Aare Slaves

Incredible as it may seem, some Jews in the labor and death camps, even during the very last stages of the Nazi "final solution," were able to bake matzah, avoid hametz, and even conduct some kind of seder. But for most of them the only element of Passover they could be certain would be present was the maror—not the symbolic bitterness of bitter herbs, but the real bitterness of actual slavery. The poignant prayer composed by the rabbis of Bergen-Belsen for those who were compelled to violate the laws of Passover may have assuaged to some degree their sense of guilt. Its poignancy is accentuated by the mold in which it is cast—that of the prayer which the pious Jew ordinarily recites when he is about to fulfill the mitzvah of eating matzah: "Behold I am prepared and ready…"

Prayer before Partaking of Hametz

Before eating hametz let him say: Our Father in heaven, it is known and revealed before Thee that it is our will to do Thy will and to observe the festival of Passover through the eating of matzah and by not violating the prohibition of hametz. For this our hearts are grieved—that our enslavement prevents us and we are in danger of our lives. Behold, then, we are prepared and ready to fulfill Thy commandment of "Thou shalt live by them and not die by them"; and to carefully heed the warning, "Take therefore good heed and guard thy life very much." Therefore it is our prayer unto Thee that Thou keep us alive and preserve us and redeem us speedily so that we may observe Thy statutes and do Thy will and serve Thee with a perfect heart. Amen."

While the Jews were still confined to the ghettos, however, and there was still some semblance of "normality," it was possible for at least some of the halakhic requirements of Passover to be complied with—this, of course, provided that halakhically sound answers could be found to the questions raised by the special circumstances which obtained in the ghetto.

Irving J Rosenbaum

Recite the following blessing, and drink the cup in the reclining position:

Blessed are You, Hashem, our God, King of the universe, who creates the fruit of the vine.

Two Concepts of Liberty

In 1958 Isaiah Berlin published what became a famous essay entitled *Two Concepts of Liberty*. In it he described first positive liberty saying,

"The 'positive' sense of the word 'liberty' derives from the wish on the part of the individual to be his own master. I wish my life and decisions to depend on myself, not on external forces of whatever kind. I wish to be the instrument of my own, not of other men's, acts of will. I wish to be a subject, not an object; to be moved by reasons, by conscious purposes, which are my own, not by causes which affect me, as it were, from outside. I wish to be somebody, not nobody; a doer - deciding, not being decided for, self-directed and not acted upon by external nature or by other men as if I were a thing, or an animal, or a slave incapable of playing a human role, that is, of conceiving goals and policies of my own and realizing them.

"Negative liberty is the absence of obstacles external to the individual. It is the absence of barriers, constraints or interference from others; external factors to the person may take the form of stop signs, societal norms or an addiction to cigarettes."

Ian Carter of Stanford University writes that negative liberty is "simply about how many doors are open to the agent" and positive liberty "is more about going through the right doors for the right reasons."

Questions:

Is the positive concept of liberty a political concept?

Can individuals / groups achieve positive freedom through political action?

Is it possible for the state to promote the positive freedom of citizens on their behalf? Those whom embrace negative freedom would answer the above as no; those who defend positive freedom would say yes.

Can a slave be free? Can you visualize that these concepts are in opposition to each other?

Personal Change

The Shemen HaTov explains that a person cannot be Holy unto himself. Even though the mitzvah is on the individual, the individual needs society's help. If one lives in a society which is indulgent, it becomes very difficult for that individual to remain a "Kadosh" [holy person].

In order to achieve "You shall be holy" (Kedoshim Tiheyu), the cooperation of one's family, of one's city and one's nation is required. Therefore, the admonition to be holy needed to be given to the entire community. When everyone is involved in conspicuous indulgence, it becomes almost impossible for the individual to act with restraint.

We see this very clearly in the society in which we live today. The rampant hedonism that we see today – gratifying their every whim and wish instantly, surrounds us. We live in a society that does not know what kedushah [holiness] is about. The only way we can personally achieve this mitzvah of "You shall be holy," is if we not only work on ourselves, but we elevate and try to live among people who also share the ideal of Kedsohim Tiheyu.

רָחְצָה

נוֹטְלִים אֶת הַיָדַיִם וּמְבָרְכִים:

בָּרוּךְ אַתָּה יְיָ אֱלֹהֵינוּ מֶלֶךְ הָעוֹלָם,
אֲשֶׁר קִדְּשָׁנוּ בְּמִצְוֹתָיו וְצִוָּנוּ עַל נְטִילַת יָדָיִם.

אֵין לְדַבֵּר עַד אֲכִילַת הַמַּצָּה.

But it must begin with the individual. As the Chassidic Rebbe, Reb Simcha Bunim of Pshis'cha (1765-1827) is quoted as having said, when he was young he thought he could change the world. As he got older, he saw that he could not change the entire world, but at least he could change his city. As time went on, he saw that even that was beyond his grasp, but he said "I'll at least change my neighborhood." When he saw that that was not working, he said "I'll at least try to change my family." When he saw that that failed, he said, "I'll have to try to only change myself."

But once he succeeded in changing himself, then he saw that his family was different, his neighborhood was different, his city was different, and in a sense the entire world was different.

That is how it is with this mitzvah of "Kedoshim Tiheyu." We cannot go it alone. We have to work on ourselves, and then on our families, and then on our neighborhoods, and then on our societies.

Rabbi Yissocher Frand

Rachtzah

Now the hands are washed with recital of the blessing for washing the hands.

Blessed are You, Hashem, our God, King of the universe, who has sanctified us with His commandments and commanded us concerning the washing of the hands.

One should not speak until after making the next 2 blessings and eating the matzah.

מוֹצִיא

לוקח את שלוש המצות – שְׁתֵּי הַשְׁלֵמוֹת וחצי המצה שביניהן – מברך "הַמּוֹצִיא". אחר כך מניח מידו את המצה התחתונה, מחזיק את המצה השלֵמה העליונה יחד עם החצויה, מברך "עַל אֲכִילַת מַצָּה", וְאוֹכֵל בַּהֲסָבָה משתי המצות – כזית מן העליונה וכזית מן החצויה (עם מעט מלח).

בָּרוּךְ אַתָּה יְיָ אֱלֹהֵינוּ מֶלֶךְ הָעוֹלָם
הַמּוֹצִיא לֶחֶם מִן הָאָרֶץ.

מַצָּה

בָּרוּךְ אַתָּה יְיָ אֱלֹהֵינוּ מֶלֶךְ הָעוֹלָם,
אֲשֶׁר קִדְּשָׁנוּ בְּמִצְוֹתָיו וְצִוָּנוּ עַל אֲכִילַת מַצָּה.

Motzi

Take the matzot in the order that they are lying on the tray – the broken piece between the two whole matzot; hold them in your hand and recite the following blessing:

Blessed are You, Hashem, our God, King of the universe, who brings forth bread from the earth.

Matzah

Do not break anything off the matzot. First put down the third matzah (the bottom one), and recite the following blessing over the broken matzah and the top one.

When reciting the following blessing, have in mind that it refers also to the eating of the "Sandwich" of **Korech** – which will be made with the third matzah – and also the eating of the **Afikoman**.

Blessed are You, Hashem, our God, King of the universe, who has sanctified us with His commandments and commanded us concerning the eating of Matzah.

Now break off a kezayit (the volume of one olive) of the 2 Matzot held, and eat the 2 pieces together in reclining position.

מָרוֹר

לוֹקֵחַ כְּזַיִת מָרוֹר, טוֹבְלוֹ בַּחֲרוֹסֶת, מְבָרֵךְ וְאוֹכֵל בְּלִי הֲסָבָה.

בָּרוּךְ אַתָּה יְיָ אֱלֹהֵינוּ מֶלֶךְ הָעוֹלָם,
אֲשֶׁר קִדְּשָׁנוּ בְּמִצְוֹתָיו וְצִוָּנוּ
עַל אֲכִילַת מָרוֹר.

כּוֹרֵךְ

Korech: Restoring Jewish Unity

The Hillel Sandwich is "bricks–and–mortar" – broken matzah held together by bitter herbs and Charoset. The matzah was once whole. So too, the Jewish people can become crushed and divisive. But we are held together by our common links to Torah and our shared historical experiences.

The Talmud says that as Jews in Egypt, we were redeemed only because of our unity. We were unified in our commitment to each other and to the future of our people. Weeks later at Mount Sinai, we stood together and accepted the Torah with one heart and one mind.

Today, we are fighting amongst ourselves under the watchful eye

כָּל אֶחָד מֵהַמְסֻבִּים לוֹקֵחַ כְּזַיִת מִן הַמַּצָּה הַשְּׁלִישִׁית עִם כְּזַיִת מָרוֹר וְכוֹרְכָם יַחַד,
אוֹכְלִים בְּהַסָבָה וּבְלִי בְּרָכָה. לִפְנֵי אֲכִלוֹ אוֹמֵר.

זֵכֶר לְמִקְדָּשׁ כְּהִלֵּל.
כֵּן עָשָׂה הִלֵּל בִּזְמַן שֶׁבֵּית הַמִּקְדָּשׁ הָיָה קַיָּם:
הָיָה כּוֹרֵךְ מַצָה וּמָרוֹר וְאוֹכֵל בְּיַחַד,
לְקַיֵּם מַה שֶׁנֶּאֱמַר: עַל מַצּוֹת וּמְרֹרִים יֹאכְלֻהוּ.

Now take a kezayit (the volume of one olive) of the maror, dip it into the charoset – but then shake off the charoset that stuck to it, so that the bitter taste will not be neutralized. Recite the following blessing, and eat without reclining:

Blessed are You, Hashem, our God, King of the universe, who has sanctified us with His commandments and commanded us concerning **the eating of Maror.**

of the world media. It is both embarrassing and discouraging. The biggest threat to Jewish survival may be from within. Our only response is to stand loudly and proclaim: Every Jew is a Jew. Period. The inclusion of the "Wicked Son" in the Seder expresses our conviction that no Jew is ever irretrievably lost. We are all one family, responsible to love and care for one another.

The matzah may be broken, but it can be restored. It is this "Hillel Sandwich" which has traditionally symbolized our commitment to glue the Jewish nation back together. On the merit of unity we were redeemed from Egypt, and it is on that merit that we shall be redeemed once again.

Rabbi Shraga Simmons

Take the third matzah, and also a kezayit (the volume of one olive) of the Chazeret – which is to be dipped into Kharoset. Combine the two [like a sandwich], and say the following and eat them together – in the reclining position:

Thus did Hilel do at the time of the Bet HaMikdash: He would combine Passover – lamb, Matzah and Maror and eat them together, as it said: "They shall eat it with Matzah and bitter herbs."

שֻׁלְחָן עוֹרֵךְ

אוֹכְלִים וְשׁוֹתִים הַסְּעוּדָה הָעֲרוּכָה וְנוֹהֲגִים לֶאֱכוֹל תְּחִלָּה בֵּיצִים מְבֻשָּׁלוֹת. וְלֹא יֹאכַל יוֹתֵר מִדַּי, שֶׁלֹּא תִהְיֶה עָלָיו אֲכִילַת אֲפִיקוֹמָן אֲכִילָה גַּסָּה.

צָפוּן

אַחַר גְּמַר הַסְּעוּדָה לוֹקֵחַ כָּל אֶחָד מֵהַמְסֻבִּים כְּזַיִת מֵהַמַּצָּה שֶׁהָיְתָה צְפוּנָה לַאֲפִיקוֹמָן וְאוֹכֵל מִמֶּנָּה כַּזַּיִת בַּהֲסִבָּה. וְצָרִיךְ לְאָכְלָהּ קֹדֶם חֲצוֹת הַלַּיְלָה.

Grateful Guests

When someone has treated you well, don't offer a cynical explanation for that person's behavior. This is the criterion used by the second century scholar Ben Zoma, to distinguish between good and bad guests. The good guest is one who thinks, "How much trouble has my host gone to for me. How much meat he set before me. How many cakes he served me. And all this trouble he has done for my sake!" The ungrateful guest regards the situation very differently: "What kind of effort did the host make for me? I have eaten only one slice of bread. I have eaten only one piece of meat, and I have drunk only one cup of wine. Whatever troubles the host went to was done only for the sake of his wife and children!" (Berachot 58a)

There are additional, perhaps even more common, ways to be an ungrateful guest. For example, many people leave a home in which they have been entertained and well treated and, even as they drive home, start criticizing and analyzing their host and his family. Such postmortems often involve speculations about the host's marital relationship, wealth, aesthetic sensibilities, taste in food, intelligence, and children's personalities. To do so is to act as a *kafui tovah*, an ingrate, toward those who have spent hours, perhaps even days, preparing and trying to make our time with them as pleasant as possible.

Rabbi Joseph Telushkin

Shulchan Orech

Now eat and drink to your heart's delight.
It is permitted to drink wine between the second and third cups.

Tzafun

After the meal, take the Afikoman and divide it among all the members of the household, by giving everyone a kezayit (the volume of one olive). Take care not to drink after the Afikoman. It is to be eaten in the reclining position and this ought to be done before midnight.

. . . .

Songs of Dreamers

... I continued reading one triumphant psalm after another: " A song of dreamers. When the Lord brought back the exiles who returned to Zion, we were like dreamers."

Yes, exactly like dreamers. But wasn't this one more dream? How many times during these years had I flown to Israel and, instead of reaching Avital, had awakened in a cold punishment cell! I was frightened, and suddenly no trace remained of the victorious self-confidence that had flooded me only a moment ago. Just then thick white clouds enveloped the pane. Yes, I thought, this really is a dream. The snowy shroud will tear open, I'll wake up, and the yellow light of the punishment – cell lamp will hit my eyes. My heart sank and a cold shiver passed over my body. Now I'll open my eyes, take the shade off the lamp, and try to warm up.

The plane burst out of the white shroud. The land was rushing toward me. Neat little homes with long slanting roofs. Hadn't I seen something like this in pictures? No it was Tallinn, in Estonia, where Avital and I once took a brief vacation. Where were we? Finland? No, not likely as we flying west the whole time. It must be Holland or Switzerland. Switzerland – of course! They had exchanged Bukovsky in Zurich!

And then the thought sank in: No matter where they release me, Avital will probably fly there. That means I'll see her soon.

Natan Sharansky
Natan Sharansky was imprisoned by the Soviet Union under the false charge of espionage. He was released in 1986.

בָּרֵךְ

מוֹזְגִין כּוֹס שְׁלִישִׁי וּמְבָרְכִין בִּרְכַּת הַמָּזוֹן.

שִׁיר הַמַּעֲלוֹת בְּשׁוּב יְיָ אֶת שִׁיבַת צִיּוֹן הָיִינוּ כְּחֹלְמִים. אָז יִמָּלֵא שְׂחוֹק פִּינוּ וּלְשׁוֹנֵנוּ רִנָּה אָז יֹאמְרוּ בַגּוֹיִם הִגְדִּיל יְיָ לַעֲשׂוֹת עִם אֵלֶּה. הִגְדִּיל יְיָ לַעֲשׂוֹת עִמָּנוּ הָיִינוּ שְׂמֵחִים. שׁוּבָה יְיָ אֶת שְׁבִיתֵנוּ כַּאֲפִיקִים בַּנֶּגֶב. הַזֹּרְעִים בְּדִמְעָה בְּרִנָּה יִקְצֹרוּ. הָלוֹךְ יֵלֵךְ וּבָכֹה נֹשֵׂא מֶשֶׁךְ הַזָּרַע בֹּא יָבוֹא בְרִנָּה נֹשֵׂא אֲלֻמֹּתָיו.
(תהלים קכ"ו)

שְׁלֹשָׁה שֶׁאָכְלוּ כְּאֶחָד חַיָּבִין לְזַמֵּן וְהַמְזַמֵּן פּוֹתֵחַ: רַבּוֹתַי, נְבָרֵךְ!

הַמְסֻבִּים עוֹנִים: יְהִי שֵׁם יְיָ מְבֹרָךְ מֵעַתָּה וְעַד עוֹלָם.

הַמְזַמֵּן אוֹמֵר: בִּרְשׁוּת מָרָנָן וְרַבָּנָן וְרַבּוֹתַי, נְבָרֵךְ (בעשרה אֱלֹהֵינוּ) שֶׁאָכַלְנוּ מִשֶּׁלּוֹ.

הַמְסֻבִּים עוֹנִים: בָּרוּךְ (אֱלֹהֵינוּ) שֶׁאָכַלְנוּ מִשֶּׁלּוֹ וּבְטוּבוֹ חָיִינוּ.

הַמְזַמֵּן חוֹזֵר וְאוֹמֵר: בָּרוּךְ (אֱלֹהֵינוּ) שֶׁאָכַלְנוּ מִשֶּׁלּוֹ וּבְטוּבוֹ חָיִינוּ.

בָּרוּךְ אַתָּה יְיָ אֱלֹהֵינוּ מֶלֶךְ הָעוֹלָם הַזָּן אֶת הָעוֹלָם כֻּלּוֹ בְּטוּבוֹ בְּחֵן בְּחֶסֶד וּבְרַחֲמִים , הוּא נוֹתֵן לֶחֶם לְכָל־בָּשָׂר כִּי לְעוֹלָם חַסְדּוֹ וּבְטוּבוֹ הַגָּדוֹל תָּמִיד לֹא חָסַר לָנוּ וְאַל יֶחְסַר לָנוּ מָזוֹן תָּמִיד לְעוֹלָם וָעֶד בַּעֲבוּר שְׁמוֹ הַגָּדוֹל כִּי הוּא אֵל זָן וּמְפַרְנֵס לַכֹּל וּמֵטִיב לַכֹּל וּמֵכִין מָזוֹן לְכָל־בְּרִיּוֹתָיו אֲשֶׁר בָּרָא
בָּרוּךְ אַתָּה יְיָ הַזָּן אֶת הַכֹּל.

נוֹדֶה לְךָ יְיָ אֱלֹהֵינוּ עַל שֶׁהִנְחַלְתָּ לַאֲבוֹתֵינוּ אֶרֶץ חֶמְדָּה טוֹבָה וּרְחָבָה וְעַל שֶׁהוֹצֵאתָנוּ יְיָ אֱלֹהֵינוּ מֵאֶרֶץ מִצְרַיִם וּפְדִיתָנוּ מִבֵּית עֲבָדִים וְעַל בְּרִיתְךָ שֶׁחָתַמְתָּ בִּבְשָׂרֵנוּ וְעַל תּוֹרָתְךָ שֶׁלִּמַּדְתָּנוּ וְעַל חֻקֶּיךָ שֶׁהוֹדַעְתָּנוּ וְעַל חַיִּים חֵן וָחֶסֶד שֶׁחוֹנַנְתָּנוּ, וְעַל אֲכִילַת מָזוֹן שֶׁחוֹנַנְתָּנוּ שָׁאַתָּה זָן וּמְפַרְנֵס אוֹתָנוּ תָּמִיד, בְּכָל יוֹם וּבְכָל עֵת וּבְכָל שָׁעָה.

erach

The third cup is poured now, and recite Birkat Hamazon (Blessing after the Meal) over it.

A Song of Ascents. When Hashem will return the exiles of Zion, we will have been like dreamers. Then our mouth will be filled with laughter, and our tongue with joyous song. Then will they say among the nations, "Hashem has done great things for these." Hashem has done great things for us, we were joyful. Hashem, return our exiles as streams in the Negev. Those who sow in tears will reap with joyous song. He goes along weeping, carrying the bag of seed; he will surely come [back] with joyous song, carrying his sheaves. (Psalms 126)

When three or more men have eaten together, one invites the others to join him in the Blessing after the Meal: **Gentlemen, let us bless.** *Everybody responds:* **May the name of Hashem be blessed from now on and forever.** *The leader repeats:* **May the name of Hashem be blessed from now on and forever.** *The leader continues:* (If there are least ten men who are participating add **"our God"**). **With the permission of the master, teachers and gentlemen let us bless (our God) for we have eaten from what is His.** *The others respond:* **Blessed be (our God) He of Whose we have eaten and through Whose goodness we live.** *The leader repeats:* **Blessed be (our God) He of Whose we have eaten and through Whose goodness we live.**

Blessed are You, Hashem, our God, King of the universe, who, in His goodness, feeds the whole world with grace, with kindness and with mercy. He gives food to all flesh, for His kindness is everlasting. Through His great goodness to us continuously we do not lack food, and may we never lack it, for the sake of His great Name. For He is a [benevolent] God who feeds and sustains all, does good to all, and prepares food for all His creatures whom He has created, as it is said: You open Your hand and satisfy the desire of every living thing. **Blessed are You Hashem, who provides food for all.**

We thank You, Hashem, our God, for having given as a heritage to our fathers a precious, good and spacious land; for having brought us out, Hashem, our God, from the land of Egypt and redeemed us from the house of slaves; for Your covenant which You have sealed in our flesh; for Your Torah which You have taught us; for Your statutes which You have made known to us; for the life, favor and kindness which You have graciously bestowed upon us; and for the food we eat with which You constantly feed and sustain us every day, at all times, and at every hour.

וְעַל הַכֹּל יְיָ אֱלֹהֵינוּ אֲנַחְנוּ מוֹדִים לָךְ וּמְבָרְכִים אוֹתָךְ, יִתְבָּרַךְ שִׁמְךָ בְּפִי כָּל חַי תָּמִיד לְעוֹלָם וָעֶד, כַּכָּתוּב: "וְאָכַלְתָּ וְשָׂבָעְתָּ, וּבֵרַכְתָּ אֶת יְיָ אֱלֹהֶיךָ עַל הָאָרֶץ הַטּוֹבָה אֲשֶׁר נָתַן לָךְ".
בָּרוּךְ אַתָּה יְיָ, עַל הָאָרֶץ וְעַל הַמָּזוֹן.

רַחֶם נָא יְיָ אֱלֹהֵינוּ עַל יִשְׂרָאֵל עַמֶּךָ, וְעַל יְרוּשָׁלַיִם עִירֶךָ, וְעַל צִיּוֹן מִשְׁכַּן כְּבוֹדֶךָ, וְעַל מַלְכוּת בֵּית דָּוִד מְשִׁיחֶךָ, וְעַל הַבַּיִת הַגָּדוֹל וְהַקָּדוֹשׁ שֶׁנִּקְרָא שִׁמְךָ עָלָיו. אֱלֹהֵינוּ, אָבִינוּ, רְעֵנוּ, זוּנֵנוּ, פַּרְנְסֵנוּ וְכַלְכְּלֵנוּ וְהַרְוִיחֵנוּ, וְהַרְוַח לָנוּ יְיָ אֱלֹהֵינוּ מְהֵרָה מִכָּל צָרוֹתֵינוּ. וְנָא אַל תַּצְרִיכֵנוּ יְיָ אֱלֹהֵינוּ, לֹא לִידֵי מַתְּנַת בָּשָׂר וָדָם וְלֹא לִידֵי הַלְוָאָתָם, כִּי אִם לְיָדְךָ הַמְּלֵאָה הַפְּתוּחָה הַקְּדוֹשָׁה וְהָרְחָבָה, שֶׁלֹּא נֵבוֹשׁ וְלֹא נִכָּלֵם לְעוֹלָם וָעֶד.

בְּשַׁבָּת מוֹסִיפִין: רְצֵה וְהַחֲלִיצֵנוּ יְיָ אֱלֹהֵינוּ בְּמִצְוֹתֶיךָ וּבְמִצְוַת יוֹם הַשְּׁבִיעִי הַשַּׁבָּת הַגָּדוֹל וְהַקָּדוֹשׁ הַזֶּה. כִּי יוֹם זֶה גָּדוֹל וְקָדוֹשׁ הוּא לְפָנֶיךָ לִשְׁבָּת בּוֹ וְלָנוּחַ בּוֹ בְּאַהֲבָה כְּמִצְוַת רְצוֹנֶךָ. וּבִרְצוֹנְךָ הָנִיחַ לָנוּ יְיָ אֱלֹהֵינוּ שֶׁלֹּא תְהֵא צָרָה וְיָגוֹן וַאֲנָחָה בְּיוֹם מְנוּחָתֵנוּ. וְהַרְאֵנוּ יְיָ אֱלֹהֵינוּ בְּנֶחָמַת צִיּוֹן עִירֶךָ וּבְבִנְיַן יְרוּשָׁלַיִם עִיר קָדְשֶׁךָ כִּי אַתָּה הוּא בַּעַל הַיְשׁוּעוֹת וּבַעַל הַנֶּחָמוֹת.

אֱלֹהֵינוּ וֵאלֹהֵי אֲבוֹתֵינוּ, יַעֲלֶה וְיָבֹא וְיַגִּיעַ וְיֵרָאֶה וְיֵרָצֶה וְיִשָּׁמַע וְיִפָּקֵד וְיִזָּכֵר זִכְרוֹנֵנוּ וּפִקְדוֹנֵנוּ, וְזִכְרוֹן אֲבוֹתֵינוּ, וְזִכְרוֹן מָשִׁיחַ בֶּן דָּוִד עַבְדֶּךָ, וְזִכְרוֹן יְרוּשָׁלַיִם עִיר קָדְשֶׁךָ, וְזִכְרוֹן כָּל עַמְּךָ בֵּית יִשְׂרָאֵל לְפָנֶיךָ, לִפְלֵיטָה לְטוֹבָה לְחֵן וּלְחֶסֶד וּלְרַחֲמִים, לְחַיִּים טוֹבִים וּלְשָׁלוֹם בְּיוֹם חַג הַמַּצּוֹת הַזֶּה זָכְרֵנוּ יְיָ אֱלֹהֵינוּ בּוֹ לְטוֹבָה וּפָקְדֵנוּ בוֹ לִבְרָכָה וְהוֹשִׁיעֵנוּ בוֹ לְחַיִּים טוֹבִים. וּבִדְבַר יְשׁוּעָה וְרַחֲמִים חוּס וְחָנֵּנוּ וְרַחֵם עָלֵינוּ וְהוֹשִׁיעֵנוּ, כִּי אֵלֶיךָ עֵינֵינוּ, כִּי אֵל מֶלֶךְ חַנּוּן וְרַחוּם אָתָּה.

וּבְנֵה יְרוּשָׁלַיִם עִיר הַקֹּדֶשׁ בִּמְהֵרָה בְיָמֵינוּ. בָּרוּךְ אַתָּה יְיָ, בּוֹנֵה בְרַחֲמָיו יְרוּשָׁלָיִם. אָמֵן.

For all this, Hashem our God, we thank You and bless You. May Your Name be blessed by the mouth of every living being, constantly and forever. As it is written: When you have eaten and are satiated, you shall bless Hashem your God, for the good land which He has given you. **Blessed are You, Hashem, for the land and for the food.**

Have mercy, God our God, upon Israel Your people, upon Jerusalem Your city, upon Zion the abode of Your glory, upon the kingship of the house of David Your anointed, and upon the great and holy House which is called by Your Name. Our God, our Father, Our Shepherd, feed us, sustain us, nourish us and give us comfort; and speedily, God our God, grant us relief from all our afflictions. Hashem, our God, please do not make us dependent upon the gifts of mortal men nor upon their loans, but only upon Your full, open, holy and generous hand, that we may not be shamed or disgraced forever and ever.

<small>On Shabbat add: May it please You, God, our God, to strengthen us through Your commandments, and through the precept of the Seventh Day, this great and holy Shabbat. For this day is great and holy before You, to refrain from work and to rest thereon with love, in accordance with the commandment of Your will. In Your will, God, our God, bestow upon us tranquility, that there shall be no trouble, sadness or grief on the day of our rest. God, our God, let us see the consolation of Zion Your city, and the rebuilding of Jerusalem Your holy city, for You are the Master of [all] salvations and the Master of [all] consolations.]</small>

Our God and God of our fathers, may there ascend, come and reach, be seen and accepted, heard, recalled and remembered before You, the remembrance and recollection of us, the remembrance of our fathers, the remembrance of Mashiach the son of David Your servant, the remembrance of Jerusalem Your holy city, and the remembrance of all Your people the House of Israel, for deliverance, well-being, grace, kindness, mercy, good life and peace, on this day of the Festival of Matzot, on this Festival of holy convocation. Remember us on this [day], Hashem, our God, for good; recollect us on this [day] for blessing; help us on this [day] for good life. With the promise of deliverance and compassion, spare us and be gracious to us; have mercy upon us and deliver us; for our eyes are directed to You, for You, God, are a gracious and merciful King.

Rebuild Jerusalem the holy city speedily in our days. Blessed are You, Hashem, who in His mercy rebuilds Jerusalem. Amen.

בָּרוּךְ אַתָּה יְיָ, אֱלֹהֵינוּ מֶלֶךְ הָעוֹלָם, הָאֵל אָבִינוּ, מַלְכֵּנוּ, אַדִירֵנוּ, בּוֹרְאֵנוּ, גּוֹאֲלֵנוּ, יוֹצְרֵנוּ, קְדוֹשֵׁנוּ קְדוֹשׁ יַעֲקֹב, רוֹעֵנוּ רוֹעֵה יִשְׂרָאֵל, הַמֶּלֶךְ הַטּוֹב וְהַמֵּטִיב לַכֹּל, שֶׁבְּכָל יוֹם וָיוֹם הוּא הֵטִיב, הוּא מֵטִיב, הוּא יֵיטִיב לָנוּ. הוּא גְמָלָנוּ הוּא גוֹמְלֵנוּ הוּא יִגְמְלֵנוּ לָעַד, לְחֵן וּלְחֶסֶד וּלְרַחֲמִים וּלְרֶוַח הַצָּלָה וְהַצְלָחָה, בְּרָכָה וִישׁוּעָה נֶחָמָה פַּרְנָסָה וְכַלְכָּלָה, וְרַחֲמִים וְחַיִּים וְשָׁלוֹם וְכָל טוֹב; וּמִכָּל טוּב לְעוֹלָם עַל יְחַסְּרֵנוּ.

הָרַחֲמָן הוּא יִמְלוֹךְ עָלֵינוּ לְעוֹלָם וָעֶד. **הָרַחֲמָן** הוּא יִתְבָּרַךְ בַּשָּׁמַיִם וּבָאָרֶץ. **הָרַחֲמָן** הוּא יִשְׁתַּבַּח לְדוֹר דּוֹרִים, וְיִתְפָּאַר בָּנוּ לָעַד וּלְנֵצַח נְצָחִים, וְיִתְהַדַּר בָּנוּ לָעַד וּלְעוֹלְמֵי עוֹלָמִים. **הָרַחֲמָן** הוּא יְפַרְנְסֵנוּ בְּכָבוֹד. **הָרַחֲמָן** הוּא יִשְׁבּוֹר עֻלֵּנוּ מֵעַל צַוָּארֵנוּ, וְהוּא יוֹלִיכֵנוּ קוֹמְמִיּוּת לְאַרְצֵנוּ. **הָרַחֲמָן** הוּא יִשְׁלַח לָנוּ בְּרָכָה מְרֻבָּה בַּבַּיִת הַזֶּה, וְעַל שֻׁלְחָן זֶה שֶׁאָכַלְנוּ עָלָיו. **הָרַחֲמָן** הוּא יִשְׁלַח לָנוּ אֶת אֵלִיָּהוּ הַנָּבִיא זָכוּר לַטּוֹב, וִיבַשֶּׂר לָנוּ בְּשׂוֹרוֹת טוֹבוֹת יְשׁוּעוֹת וְנֶחָמוֹת.

בבית אביו אומר: **הָרַחֲמָן** הוּא יְבָרֵךְ אֶת אָבִי מוֹרִי בַּעַל הַבַּיִת הַזֶּה, וְאֶת אִמִּי מוֹרָתִי בַּעֲלַת הַבַּיִת הַזֶּה. נשוי אומר: **הָרַחֲמָן** הוּא יְבָרֵךְ אוֹתִי, (אם אביו ואמו בחיים: וְאֶת אָבִי מוֹרִי, וְאֶת אִמִּי מוֹרָתִי,) וְאֶת אִשְׁתִּי, וְאֶת זַרְעִי, וְאֶת כָּל אֲשֶׁר לִי. אשה נשואה אומרת: **הָרַחֲמָן** הוּא יְבָרֵךְ אוֹתִי, (אם אביה ואמה בחיים: וְאֶת אָבִי מוֹרִי, וְאֶת אִמִּי מוֹרָתִי,) וְאֶת בַּעֲלִי, וְאֶת זַרְעִי, וְאֶת כָּל אֲשֶׁר לִי. אורח אומר: **הָרַחֲמָן** הוּא יְבָרֵךְ אֶת בַּעַל הַבַּיִת הַזֶּה וְאֶת בַּעֲלַת הַבַּיִת הַזֶּה, אוֹתָם וְאֶת בֵּיתָם וְאֶת זַרְעָם וְאֶת כָּל אֲשֶׁר לָהֶם.

אוֹתָנוּ וְאֶת כָּל אֲשֶׁר לָנוּ, כְּמוֹ שֶׁנִּתְבָּרְכוּ אֲבוֹתֵינוּ אַבְרָהָם יִצְחָק וְיַעֲקֹב "בַּכֹּל"–"מִכֹּל"–"כֹּל" – כֵּן יְבָרֵךְ אוֹתָנוּ כֻּלָּנוּ יַחַד בִּבְרָכָה שְׁלֵמָה. וְנֹאמַר: "אָמֵן".

Blessed are You, Hashem, our God, King of the universe, benevolent God, our Father, our King, our Might, our Creator, our Redeemer, our Maker, our Holy One, the Holy One of Jacob, our Shepherd, the Shepherd of Israel, the King who is good and does good to all, each and every day. He has done good for us, He does good for us, and He will do good for us; He has bestowed, He bestows, and He will forever bestow upon us grace, kindness and mercy, relief, salvation and success, blessing and help, consolation, sustenance and nourishment, compassion, life, peace and all goodness; and may He never cause us to lack any good.

May the Merciful One bless (my father, my teacher) the master of this house, and (my mother, my teacher) lady of this house, me (my wife/husband and family) and all that is mine, and all that sit here; them, their house, their family, and all that is theirs, ours and all that is ours – just as our forefathers Abraham, Isaac, and Jacob were blessed in everything, from everything, with everything. So may He bless us all together with a perfect blessing. And let us say: Amen!

Those eating at their own table recite and add the appropriate insertions:

The compassionate One. May He bless me (my wife/husband and my children) **and all that is mine**

Children at the table of their parents include the words in parenthesis:

The compassionate One. May He bless (my father, my teacher) **the master of this house, and** (my mother my teacher) **lady of this house, them, their house, their family and all that is theirs.**

Ours and all that is ours, just as our forefathers Abraham, Issac and Jacob were blessed in everything, from everything, So may He bless us all together with a perfect blessing. And let us say: Amen.

בַּמָּרוֹם יְלַמְּדוּ עֲלֵיהֶם וְעָלֵינוּ זְכוּת שֶׁתְּהֵא לְמִשְׁמֶרֶת שָׁלוֹם. וְנִשָּׂא בְרָכָה מֵאֵת יְיָ, וּצְדָקָה מֵאֱלֹהֵי יִשְׁעֵנוּ, וְנִמְצָא חֵן וְשֵׂכֶל טוֹב בְּעֵינֵי אֱלֹהִים וְאָדָם.

בשבת: **הָרַחֲמָן** הוּא יַנְחִילֵנוּ יוֹם שֶׁכֻּלּוֹ שַׁבָּת וּמְנוּחָה לְחַיֵּי הָעוֹלָמִים. **הָרַחֲמָן** הוּא יַנְחִילֵנוּ יוֹם שֶׁכֻּלּוֹ טוֹב. **הָרַחֲמָן** הוּא יְזַכֵּנוּ לִימוֹת הַמָּשִׁיחַ וּלְחַיֵּי הָעוֹלָם הַבָּא.

מִגְדּוֹל יְשׁוּעוֹת מַלְכּוֹ, וְעֹשֶׂה חֶסֶד לִמְשִׁיחוֹ, לְדָוִד וּלְזַרְעוֹ עַד עוֹלָם. עֹשֶׂה שָׁלוֹם בִּמְרוֹמָיו, הוּא יַעֲשֶׂה שָׁלוֹם עָלֵינוּ וְעַל כָּל יִשְׂרָאֵל. וְאִמְרוּ: "אָמֵן".

יְראוּ אֶת יְיָ קְדֹשָׁיו, כִּי אֵין מַחְסוֹר לִירֵאָיו. כְּפִירִים רָשׁוּ וְרָעֵבוּ, וְדֹרְשֵׁי יְיָ לֹא יַחְסְרוּ כָל טוֹב. הוֹדוּ לַיְיָ כִּי טוֹב, כִּי לְעוֹלָם חַסְדּוֹ. פּוֹתֵחַ אֶת יָדֶךָ, וּמַשְׂבִּיעַ לְכָל חַי רָצוֹן. בָּרוּךְ הַגֶּבֶר אֲשֶׁר יִבְטַח בַּיְיָ, וְהָיָה יְיָ מִבְטַחוֹ. נַעַר הָיִיתִי גַם זָקַנְתִּי, וְלֹא רָאִיתִי צַדִּיק נֶעֱזָב, וְזַרְעוֹ מְבַקֶּשׁ לָחֶם. יְיָ עֹז לְעַמּוֹ יִתֵּן, יְיָ יְבָרֵךְ אֶת עַמּוֹ בַשָּׁלוֹם.

כּוֹס שְׁלִישִׁית

הִנְנִי מוּכָן וּמְזֻמָּן לְקַיֵּם מִצְוַת כּוֹס שְׁלִישִׁי שֶׁהוּא כְּנֶגֶד בְּשׂוֹרַת הַיְשׁוּעָה, שֶׁאָמַר הַקָּדוֹשׁ בָּרוּךְ הוּא לְיִשְׂרָאֵל וְגָאַלְתִּי אֶתְכֶם בִּזְרוֹעַ נְטוּיָה וּבִשְׁפָטִים גְּדוֹלִים.

בָּרוּךְ אַתָּה יְיָ אֱלֹהֵינוּ מֶלֶךְ הָעוֹלָם בּוֹרֵא פְּרִי הַגָּפֶן.

שׁוֹתִין בַּהֲסִבַּת שְׂמֹאל.

מוֹזְגִין כּוֹס רְבִיעִי.

From On High, may there be invoked upon him and upon us such merit which will bring a safeguarding of peace. May we receive blessing from the God and just kindness from the God of our salvation, and may we find grace and good understanding in the eyes of God and man.

(On Shabbat add: **May the Merciful One** cause us to inherit that day which will be all Shabbat and rest for life everlasting.) **May the Merciful One** cause us to inherit that day which is all good. **May the Merciful One** grant us the privilege of reaching the days of the Mashiach and the life of the World to Come.

He is a tower of salvation to His king, and bestows kindness upon His anointed, to David and his descendants forever. He who makes peace in His heights, may He make peace for us and for all Israel; and say, Amen.

Fear Hashem, you His holy ones, for those who fear Him suffer no want. Young lions are in need and go hungry, but those who seek Hashem shall not lack any good. Give thanks to Hashem for He is good, for His kindness is everlasting. You open Your hand and satisfy the desire of every living thing. Blessed is the man who trusts in Hashem, and Hashem will be his trust.

The Third Cup

Recite the blessing for the wine.

Blessed are You, Hashem, our God, King of the universe, who creates the fruit of the vine.

Drink while reclining to the left.

The fourth cup is poured

For One Brief Moment the Jew Stood Tall

Many Seder participants are decidedly uncomfortable with the short paragraph which asks that God's wrath be poured out on the nations that do not call out in God's name.

Some modern Haggadot deleted this paragraph, finding it too pregnant with vengeance and revenge. Defying the Seder's universal themes of freedom and liberation, it made their compilers uncomfortable. I, on the other hand, love it. Why my infatuation with this hard-hitting paragraph?

I picture the many beleaguered Jews, particularly In Europe, for whom Passover, with its proximity to Easter, was a dangerous time. I imagine Jews who spent much of the year fearful that the non-Jewish world might violently turn on them. They knew they would have little recourse to protect themselves...

פּוֹתְחִים הַדֶּלֶת וְאוֹמְרִים בְּקוֹל רָם

שְׁפֹךְ חֲמָתְךָ

אֶל הַגּוֹיִם אֲשֶׁר לֹא יְדָעוּךָ
וְעַל מַמְלָכוֹת אֲשֶׁר בְּשִׁמְךָ לֹא קָרָאוּ.
כִּי אָכַל אֶת יַעֲקֹב וְאֶת נָוֵהוּ הֵשַׁמּוּ.
שְׁפֹךְ עֲלֵיהֶם זַעְמֶךָ וַחֲרוֹן אַפְּךָ יַשִּׂיגֵם.
תִּרְדֹּף בְּאַף וְתַשְׁמִידֵם מִתַּחַת שְׁמֵי יְיָ.

סוֹגְרִים הַדֶּלֶת

Suddenly, for one short paragraph, they opened the door of their homes – of course, most of their non-Jewish neighbors had by then retired for the night – and publicly told the world what they wished for those who had done them evil. For one brief moment they could let their desire for justice be heard publicly. They did not have to cower in fear.

And yet they did not ask God to let them pour out their own wrath. Even now when Jewish "machismo" briefly appeared, they asked God to render judgment and to punish only those who did not "call out in God's name," that is, those nations that failed to adhere to ethical standards. For one brief, shining moment, the Jew stood tall. The playing field was more than equal as the Jew turned to the Judge of all the world, the same Judge Abraham challenged in Genesis, and called upon that Judge to do justice. And then, as suddenly as it began, it ended. The door was shut, the Jew sat down, the Seder continued, and all returned as it had been and would remain for too many years.

Deborah E. Lipstadt

The door is opened. Say the following:

Pour out Your wrath

upon the nations that do not acknowledge You, and upon the kingdoms that do not call upon Your Name. For they have devoured Jacob and laid waste his habitation. Pour out Your indignation upon them, and let the wrath of Your anger overtake them. Pursue them with anger, and destroy them from beneath the heavens of Hashem.

The door is closed.

> ### Israel, the Realized Dream
> Israel's antecedents were the religious ideals and institutions of a dispersed people, the cataclysmic events of the preceding 100 years..., 19th & 20th international political developments, heroic pioneer movements and trail-blazing individuals, the philosophic speculation and creative experimentation of men of genius, and the outcome of specific struggles and momentous crises. Though comparatively small in area and population, the land of Israel... has been both the centrifugal and centripetal force for world Jewry – when Israel was the romance of the past and the dream of the future, and now that it has become a reality of the present.

הַלֵּל

לֹא לָנוּ יְיָ לֹא לָנוּ, כִּי לְשִׁמְךָ תֵּן כָּבוֹד, עַל חַסְדְּךָ, עַל אֲמִתֶּךָ. לָמָּה יֹאמְרוּ הַגּוֹיִם אַיֵּה נָא אֱלֹהֵיהֶם, וֵאלֹהֵינוּ בַשָּׁמָיִם, כֹּל אֲשֶׁר חָפֵץ עָשָׂה. עֲצַבֵּיהֶם כֶּסֶף וְזָהָב מַעֲשֵׂה יְדֵי אָדָם. פֶּה לָהֶם וְלֹא יְדַבֵּרוּ, עֵינַיִם לָהֶם וְלֹא יִרְאוּ. אָזְנַיִם לָהֶם וְלֹא יִשְׁמָעוּ, אַף לָהֶם וְלֹא יְרִיחוּן. יְדֵיהֶם וְלֹא יְמִישׁוּן, רַגְלֵיהֶם וְלֹא יְהַלֵּכוּ, לֹא יֶהְגּוּ בִּגְרוֹנָם. כְּמוֹהֶם יִהְיוּ עֹשֵׂיהֶם, כֹּל אֲשֶׁר בֹּטֵחַ בָּהֶם.

יִשְׂרָאֵל בְּטַח בַּייָ, עֶזְרָם וּמָגִנָּם הוּא.
בֵּית אַהֲרֹן בִּטְחוּ בַייָ, עֶזְרָם וּמָגִנָּם הוּא.
יִרְאֵי יְיָ בִּטְחוּ בַייָ, עֶזְרָם וּמָגִנָּם הוּא.

> A people that has made a signal contribution to the spiritual growth of mankind merits singular attention when it reconstitutes itself on its ancient soil and resumes the cultivation of human and universal values. Out of the matrix of a new and vibrant society, there may come innovations and insights that will benefit all civilization. Certainly, the one bastion of democracy in Middle East despotism, the one island of enlightenment in a Levantine sea of ignorance and strife, is destined to benefit its geographic periphery... the Jew on the American scene... remains knowingly or unwittingly conditioned by the Zionist vision, as revealed and realized in Israel today... The stigma of homelessness is replaced by the banner of national sovereignty.
>
> **Gershon Winer**

Hallel

Not to us, Hashem, not to us, but to Your Name give glory, for the sake of Your kindness and Your truth. Why should the nations say, "Where, now, is their God?" Our God is in heaven, whatever He desires, He does. Their idols are of silver and gold, the product of human hands: they have a mouth, but cannot speak; they have eyes, but cannot see; they have ears, but cannot hear; they have a nose, but cannot smell; their hands cannot feel; their feet cannot walk; they can make no sound with their throat. Like them should be their makers, everyone that trusts in them. Israel, trust in Hashem! He is their help and their shield. House of Aaron, trust in Hashem! He is their help and their shield. You who fear Hashem, trust in Hashem! He is their help and their shield.

יְיָ זְכָרָנוּ יְבָרֵךְ, יְבָרֵךְ אֶת בֵּית יִשְׂרָאֵל, יְבָרֵךְ אֶת בֵּית אַהֲרֹן. יְבָרֵךְ יִרְאֵי יְיָ, הַקְּטַנִּים עִם הַגְּדֹלִים. יֹסֵף יְיָ עֲלֵיכֶם, עֲלֵיכֶם וְעַל בְּנֵיכֶם. בְּרוּכִים אַתֶּם לַיְיָ, עֹשֵׂה שָׁמַיִם וָאָרֶץ. הַשָּׁמַיִם שָׁמַיִם לַיְיָ וְהָאָרֶץ נָתַן לִבְנֵי אָדָם. לֹא הַמֵּתִים יְהַלְלוּ יָהּ וְלֹא כָּל יֹרְדֵי דוּמָה. וַאֲנַחְנוּ נְבָרֵךְ יָהּ מֵעַתָּה וְעַד עוֹלָם. **הַלְלוּיָהּ:**

אָהַבְתִּי כִּי יִשְׁמַע יְיָ אֶת קוֹלִי, תַּחֲנוּנָי. כִּי הִטָּה אָזְנוֹ לִי וּבְיָמַי אֶקְרָא. אֲפָפוּנִי חֶבְלֵי מָוֶת וּמְצָרֵי שְׁאוֹל מְצָאוּנִי, צָרָה וְיָגוֹן אֶמְצָא. וּבְשֵׁם יְיָ אֶקְרָא, אָנָּא יְיָ מַלְּטָה נַפְשִׁי. חַנּוּן יְיָ וְצַדִּיק, וֵאלֹהֵינוּ מְרַחֵם. שֹׁמֵר פְּתָאיִם יְיָ, דַּלּוֹתִי וְלִי יְהוֹשִׁיעַ. שׁוּבִי נַפְשִׁי לִמְנוּחָיְכִי, כִּי יְיָ גָּמַל עָלָיְכִי. כִּי חִלַּצְתָּ נַפְשִׁי מִמָּוֶת, אֶת עֵינִי מִן דִּמְעָה, אֶת רַגְלִי מִדֶּחִי. אֶתְהַלֵּךְ לִפְנֵי יְיָ בְּאַרְצוֹת הַחַיִּים. הֶאֱמַנְתִּי כִּי אֲדַבֵּר, אֲנִי עָנִיתִי מְאֹד. אֲנִי אָמַרְתִּי בְחָפְזִי, כָּל הָאָדָם כֹּזֵב.

מָה אָשִׁיב לַיְיָ כָּל תַּגְמוּלוֹהִי עָלָי. כּוֹס יְשׁוּעוֹת אֶשָּׂא וּבְשֵׁם יְיָ אֶקְרָא. נְדָרַי לַיְיָ אֲשַׁלֵּם נֶגְדָה נָּא לְכָל עַמּוֹ. יָקָר בְּעֵינֵי יְיָ הַמָּוְתָה לַחֲסִידָיו. אָנָּא יְיָ כִּי אֲנִי עַבְדֶּךָ, אֲנִי עַבְדְּךָ בֶּן אֲמָתֶךָ, פִּתַּחְתָּ לְמוֹסֵרָי. לְךָ אֶזְבַּח זֶבַח תּוֹדָה וּבְשֵׁם יְיָ אֶקְרָא. נְדָרַי לַיְיָ אֲשַׁלֵּם נֶגְדָה נָּא לְכָל עַמּוֹ. בְּחַצְרוֹת בֵּית יְיָ, בְּתוֹכֵכִי יְרוּשָׁלָיִם, הַלְלוּיָהּ:

Hashem, mindful of us, will bless. He will bless the House of Israel; He will bless the House of Aaron; He will bless those who fear Hashem, the small with the great. May Hashem increase [blessing] upon you, upon you and upon your children. You are blessed unto Hashem, the Maker of heaven and earth. The heavens are the heavens of Hashem, but the earth He gave to the children of man. The dead do not praise God, nor do those that go down into the silence [of the grave]. But we will bless God, from now to eternity. Halleluyah Praise God.

I love Hashem, because He hears my voice, my prayers. For He turned His ear to me; all my days I will call [upon Him]. The pangs of death encompassed me, and the agonies of the grave came upon me, trouble and sorrow I encounter and I call upon the Name of Hashem: Please, God, deliver my soul! Hashem is gracious and just, our God is compassionate. Hashem watches over the simpletons; I was brought low and He saved me. Return, my soul, to your rest, for Hashem has dealt kindly with you. For You have delivered my soul from death, my eyes from tears, my foot from stumbling. I will walk before Hashem in the lands of the living. I had faith even when I said, "I am greatly afflicted;" [even when] I said in my haste, "All men are deceitful."

What can I repay Hashem for all His kindness to me? I will raise the cup of salvation and call upon the Name of Hashem. I will pay my vows to Hashem in the presence of all His people. Precious in the eyes of Hashem is the death of His pious ones. I thank you, God, for I am Your servant. I am Your servant the son of Your handmaid, You have loosened my bonds. To You I will bring an offering of thanksgiving, and I will call upon the Name of Hashem. I will pay my vows to Hashem in the presence of all His people, in the courtyards of the House of Hashem, in the midst of Jerusalem. Halleluyah Praise God.

The Exodus and Aliya – Introduction and Personal Narrative

The naval operations of the Hagana (the military arm of the Jewish community in British–ruled Eretz Israel – Palestine) revolved around Aliya Bet – the large-scale enterprise to bring ma'apilim (illegal immigrants) to Eretz Israel during the British Mandate, in defiance of British policies that severely limited Jewish immigration.

Within the Hagana were the elite forces known as the Palmach and within the Palmach the forces assigned to naval activities was known as the Palyam.

The four biggest ships of Aliya Bet – Exodus 1947, Knesset Israel and the two Pan's that together carried 23,600 people, carried about one third of all the ma'apilim of Aliya Bet after WW–II. Exodus and Knesset Israel were also the battlegrounds of two of the more bitter clashes with British forces during Aliya Bet, resulting in a few casualties and hundreds of wounded. The especially moving and unique story of the Exodus resulted in her being the flagship and undisputed symbol of Aliya Bet.

I was born in a small town near Krakow, Poland, to a Zionist-oriented family, and was active in the Hashomer Hatzair Youth Org.

In 1942, I joined the Palmach and was accepted into the second course for small boat commanders and was assigned to a refugee carrier called the "Amos." When the immigrants had been helped off the ship at Shefayim [a Kibbutz located on the Mediterranean coast about ten miles north of Tel Aviv], a British destroyer caught the last two small boatloads of immigrants while still in the water. I was in charge of one of these boats. All of us were arrested and incarcerated at the Latrun prison camp. For me and for most of the other Palyamniks, this was our first meeting with the remnant of the Holocaust. This was what was left of the Jews of Greece who survived the death camps. As Alterman wrote: "They carried the nation on their shoulders." That is exactly how it was and how we felt.

I was eventually released from prison and reassigned to a former ice breaking ship called the Northland. Among the passengers there were 150 babies that were carried by their mothers in little wicker baskets onto the ship. We housed them all in what we had designated as the hospital ward, and their mothers slept not far from them so that they could take care of them during the voyage. We now carried 2,664 Olim.

As we approached Haifa we changed the names of the ship to their Hagana names, as instructed by headquarters in Tel Aviv. The

"Northland" became "The Jewish State." The name was painted in large letters on the bridges of the ships, in English and in Hebrew.

On the morning of the 2nd of October, while approaching the shores of Palestine, we on the "Northland" made for Tel Aviv. Soon, the two British destroyers that accompanied us from our origin in Romania were joined by two more, so that we had an entourage of four destroyers, two on each side accompanying us. The "Geula" was not neglected either and also noted an increase in the number of destroyers that gathered. A process of trying to convince us now took place in Yiddish, Romanian, and Hebrew. When talking did not help, they sprayed streams of water on the decks as well as tear gas. They then tried to tie up alongside us but we managed to maneuver to prevent them from so doing. Finally toward evening they tried again to come alongside but we turned the bow of the ship toward them and crashed into them. The destroyer on our port side was damaged by this collision but the destroyer on the starboard side managed to secure a hold and a squad of armed marines boarded the ship and captured the bridge. We had previously disconnected control of the helm from the bridge, and controlled the ship's movements from the helm in the hold below deck. The "Jewish State" had been an ice–breaker so it had not been damaged by the collision. None of the immigrants were hurt because we were able to warn them of the collision in advance and they were prepared for it. We continued to move to the coast with the British destroyer alongside us and the lights of Tel Aviv were seen in the distance as evening descended. A strong force of British sailors boarded the ship and forced its way to the engine room and managed to put the engines out of commission. We now had no electricity and no air in the holds so we told everyone to go up on deck. The destroyer towed us into Haifa, and we arrived there the following morning. We were moored once more alongside the "Geula" at what the poet Alterman called the "Pier of Tears."

This is where all the ships captured by the British fleet were kept in a corner of the port. We stayed on board for three days. The conditions on the ship were very difficult and we were kept there because the British were debating if they should do another "Exodus" and send us back to Europe, or to find another alternative. In the end, we were sent to Cyprus and not sent back to Europe.

Yosef Almog

הַלְלוּ אֶת יְיָ כָּל גּוֹיִם, שַׁבְּחוּהוּ כָּל הָאֻמִּים. כִּי גָבַר עָלֵינוּ חַסְדּוֹ, וֶאֱמֶת יְיָ לְעוֹלָם, הַלְלוּיָהּ:

הוֹדוּ לַייָ כִּי טוֹב, כִּי לְעוֹלָם חַסְדּוֹ.
יֹאמַר נָא יִשְׂרָאֵל, כִּי לְעוֹלָם חַסְדּוֹ.
יֹאמְרוּ נָא בֵית אַהֲרֹן, כִּי לְעוֹלָם חַסְדּוֹ.
יֹאמְרוּ נָא יִרְאֵי יְיָ, כִּי לְעוֹלָם חַסְדּוֹ.

מִן הַמֵּצַר קָרָאתִי יָּהּ, עָנָנִי בַמֶּרְחָב יָהּ.
יְיָ לִי לֹא אִירָא, מַה יַּעֲשֶׂה לִי אָדָם. יְיָ לִי בְּעֹזְרָי וַאֲנִי אֶרְאֶה בְשֹׂנְאָי. טוֹב לַחֲסוֹת בַּייָ מִבְּטֹחַ בָּאָדָם.
טוֹב לַחֲסוֹת בַּייָ מִבְּטֹחַ בִּנְדִיבִים.
כָּל גּוֹיִם סְבָבוּנִי, בְּשֵׁם יְיָ כִּי אֲמִילַם. סַבּוּנִי גַם סְבָבוּנִי, בְּשֵׁם יְיָ כִּי אֲמִילַם. סַבּוּנִי כִדְבוֹרִים, דֹּעֲכוּ כְּאֵשׁ קוֹצִים, בְּשֵׁם יְיָ כִּי אֲמִילַם. דָּחֹה דְחִיתַנִי לִנְפֹּל, וַייָ עֲזָרָנִי.
עָזִּי וְזִמְרָת יָהּ וַיְהִי לִי לִישׁוּעָה.
קוֹל רִנָּה וִישׁוּעָה בְּאָהֳלֵי צַדִּיקִים, יְמִין יְיָ עֹשָׂה חָיִל.
יְמִין יְיָ רוֹמֵמָה, יְמִין יְיָ עֹשָׂה חָיִל.
לֹא אָמוּת כִּי אֶחְיֶה, וַאֲסַפֵּר מַעֲשֵׂי יָהּ.
יַסֹּר יִסְּרַנִּי יָּהּ, וְלַמָּוֶת לֹא נְתָנָנִי.
פִּתְחוּ לִי שַׁעֲרֵי צֶדֶק, אָבֹא בָם, אוֹדֶה יָהּ.
זֶה הַשַּׁעַר לַייָ, צַדִּיקִים יָבֹאוּ בוֹ.

Praise Hashem, all nations! Extol Him, all peoples! For His kindness was mighty over us, and the truth of Hashem is everlasting. Halleluyah Praise God.

Give thanks to Hashem, for He is good, **for His kindness is everlasting.** Let Israel say [it], **for His kindness is everlasting.** Let the House of Aaron say [it], **for His kindness is everlasting.** Let those who fear Hashem say [it], **for His kindness is everlasting.**

Out of narrow confines I called to God; God answered me with abounding relief. Hashem is with me, I will not fear what can man do to me? Hashem is with me, through my helpers, and I can face my enemies. It is better to rely on Hashem, than to trust in man. It is better to rely on Hashem, than to trust in nobles. All nations surround me, but I cut them down in the Name of Hashem. They surrounded me, they encompassed me, but I cut them down in the Name of Hashem. They surrounded me like bees, yet they are extinguished like a fire of thorns; I cut them down in the Name of Hashem. You [my foes] pushed me again and again to fall, but Hashem helped me. God is my strength and song, and this has been my salvation. The sound of joyous song and salvation is in the tents of the righteous: "The right hand of Hashem performs deeds of valor. The right hand of Hashem is exalted; the right hand of Hashem performs deeds of valor!" I shall not die, but I shall live and relate the deeds of God. God has chastised me, but He did not give me over to death. Open for me the gates of righteousness; I will enter them and give thanks to God. This is the gate of Hashem, the righteous will enter it.

אוֹדְךָ כִּי עֲנִיתָנִי וַתְּהִי לִי לִישׁוּעָה.
אוֹדְךָ כִּי עֲנִיתָנִי וַתְּהִי לִי לִישׁוּעָה.

אֶבֶן מָאֲסוּ הַבּוֹנִים הָיְתָה לְרֹאשׁ פִּנָּה.
אֶבֶן מָאֲסוּ הַבּוֹנִים הָיְתָה לְרֹאשׁ פִּנָּה.

מֵאֵת יְיָ הָיְתָה זֹּאת הִיא נִפְלָאת בְּעֵינֵינוּ.
מֵאֵת יְיָ הָיְתָה זֹּאת הִיא נִפְלָאת בְּעֵינֵינוּ.

זֶה הַיּוֹם עָשָׂה יְיָ נָגִילָה וְנִשְׂמְחָה בוֹ.
זֶה הַיּוֹם עָשָׂה יְיָ נָגִילָה וְנִשְׂמְחָה בוֹ.

אָנָּא יְיָ, הוֹשִׁיעָה נָּא.   אָנָּא יְיָ, הוֹשִׁיעָה נָּא.
אָנָּא יְיָ, הַצְלִיחָה נָא.   אָנָּא יְיָ, הַצְלִיחָה נָא.

בָּרוּךְ הַבָּא בְּשֵׁם יְיָ, בֵּרַכְנוּכֶם מִבֵּית יְיָ.
בָּרוּךְ הַבָּא בְּשֵׁם יְיָ, בֵּרַכְנוּכֶם מִבֵּית יְיָ.

אֵל יְיָ וַיָּאֶר לָנוּ. אִסְרוּ חַג בַּעֲבֹתִים עַד קַרְנוֹת הַמִּזְבֵּחַ.
אֵל יְיָ וַיָּאֶר לָנוּ. אִסְרוּ חַג בַּעֲבֹתִים עַד קַרְנוֹת הַמִּזְבֵּחַ.

אֵלִי אַתָּה וְאוֹדֶךָּ, אֱלֹהַי אֲרוֹמְמֶךָּ.
אֵלִי אַתָּה וְאוֹדֶךָּ, אֱלֹהַי אֲרוֹמְמֶךָּ.

הוֹדוּ לַיְיָ כִּי טוֹב, כִּי לְעוֹלָם חַסְדּוֹ.
הוֹדוּ לַיְיָ כִּי טוֹב, כִּי לְעוֹלָם חַסְדּוֹ.

יְהַלְלוּךָ יְיָ אֱלֹהֵינוּ כָּל מַעֲשֶׂיךָ, וַחֲסִידֶיךָ צַדִּיקִים עוֹשֵׂי רְצוֹנֶךָ, וְכָל עַמְּךָ בֵּית יִשְׂרָאֵל בְּרִנָּה יוֹדוּ וִיבָרְכוּ, וִישַׁבְּחוּ וִיפָאֲרוּ, וִירוֹמְמוּ וְיַעֲרִיצוּ, וְיַקְדִּישׁוּ וְיַמְלִיכוּ אֶת שִׁמְךָ,

I thank You for You have answered me, and You have been a help to me. (Repeat this verse)

The stone scorned by the builders has become the main cornerstone (Repeat this verse).

This was indeed from Hashem, it is wondrous in our eyes (Repeat this verse).

This day Hashem has made, let us be glad and rejoice on it (Repeat this verse).

O Hashem, please help us!   O Hashem, please help us!
O Hashem, please grant us success!   O Hashem, please grant us success!

Blessed is he who comes in the Name of Hashem; we bless you from the House of Hashem. (Repeat this verse)

Hashem is Almighty, He gave us light; bind the festival-offering until [you bring it to] the horns of the altar. (Repeat this verse)

You are my God and I will thank You; my God, I will exalt You. (Repeat this verse)

Give thanks to Hashem, for He is good, for His kindness is everlasting. (Repeat this verse)

Hashem, our God, all Your works shall praise You; Your pious ones, the righteous who do Your will, and all Your people, the House of Israel, with joyous song will thank and bless, laud and glorify, exalt and adore, sanctify and proclaim the sovereignty of

מַלְכֵּנוּ. כִּי לְךָ טוֹב לְהוֹדוֹת וּלְשִׁמְךָ נָאֶה לְזַמֵּר,
כִּי מֵעוֹלָם וְעַד עוֹלָם אַתָּה אֵל.

The Redemption/Transformation Debate

So when exactly were the Jews freed from Egypt? When they were notified that exodus was imminent with the personal actions they may have taken, such as putting the blood on their doors and eating the first ever Passover sacrifice? Or when they actually picked up and left in the morning?

This issue bothered the rabbis from the time of the Mishna (circa 300 C.E) when they debated when the redemption of the Jews from Egypt took place. And thus the Rabbis have said in the Sifre: Did not the Jews go out of Egypt only at daytime, as it is said, *On the morrow after the Passover the children of Israel went out?* How is it then that the Scripture says that we were brought forth out of Egypt by night?

Simply, this teaches us that the redemption [from bondage] took place at night [although the actual exodus took place during the day]." And in the Gemara of Tractate Berachoth we read: "All agree that the redemption took place at night, as it is said, *The Eternal thy God brought thee forth out of Egypt by night*, but the actual going forth took place only at daytime, as it is said, *On the morrow after the Passover the children of Israel went with a high hand in the sight of the all the Egyptians.*"

When does an individual become a changed person? At the inception of the idea and perhaps at the beginning of the implementation of change? Or only after achieving measurable and concrete change?

Your Name, our King. For it is good to thank You, and befitting to sing to Your Name, for from the beginning to the end of the world You are Almighty God. Give thanks to Hashem, for He is good for His kindness is everlasting;

Choose Life!

"הַעִדֹתִי בָכֶם הַיּוֹם אֶת הַשָּׁמַיִם וְאֶת הָאָרֶץ הַחַיִּים וְהַמָּוֶת נָתַתִּי לְפָנֶיךָ הַבְּרָכָה וְהַקְּלָלָה וּבָחַרְתָּ בַּחַיִּים לְמַעַן תִּחְיֶה אַתָּה וְזַרְעֶךָ" I call heaven and earth today to bear witness against you: I have placed life and death before you, blessing and curse; and you shall choose life, so that you will live, you and your offspring.

You shall choose life. The Torah stresses that the choice of life is not only for the benefit of the one making the choice, but also so that the offspring shall live. This implies that one should choose in such a way that one's offspring as well will be inspired to follow the Torah. If a person obeys the commandments half-heartedly or with the attitude that they are a heavy burden, his children will naturally be reluctant to obey them. But if he studies the Torah and carries out its precepts with joy and pride, his example will carry over to others.

Rabbi Moshe Feinstein

הוֹדוּ לַיְיָ כִּי טוֹב כִּי לְעוֹלָם חַסְדּוֹ.
הוֹדוּ לֵאלֹהֵי הָאֱלֹהִים כִּי לְעוֹלָם חַסְדּוֹ.
הוֹדוּ לַאֲדֹנֵי הָאֲדֹנִים כִּי לְעוֹלָם חַסְדּוֹ.
לְעֹשֵׂה נִפְלָאוֹת גְּדֹלוֹת לְבַדּוֹ כִּי לְעוֹלָם חַסְדּוֹ.
לְעֹשֵׂה הַשָּׁמַיִם בִּתְבוּנָה כִּי לְעוֹלָם חַסְדּוֹ.
לְרוֹקַע הָאָרֶץ עַל הַמָּיִם כִּי לְעוֹלָם חַסְדּוֹ.
לְעֹשֵׂה אוֹרִים גְּדֹלִים כִּי לְעוֹלָם חַסְדּוֹ.
אֶת הַשֶּׁמֶשׁ לְמֶמְשֶׁלֶת בַּיּוֹם כִּי לְעוֹלָם חַסְדּוֹ.
אֶת הַיָּרֵחַ וְכוֹכָבִים לְמֶמְשְׁלוֹת בַּלָּיְלָה כִּי לְעוֹלָם חַסְדּוֹ.
לְמַכֵּה מִצְרַיִם בִּבְכוֹרֵיהֶם כִּי לְעוֹלָם חַסְדּוֹ.
וַיּוֹצֵא יִשְׂרָאֵל מִתּוֹכָם כִּי לְעוֹלָם חַסְדּוֹ.
בְּיָד חֲזָקָה וּבִזְרוֹעַ נְטוּיָה כִּי לְעוֹלָם חַסְדּוֹ.
לְגֹזֵר יַם סוּף לִגְזָרִים כִּי לְעוֹלָם חַסְדּוֹ.
וְהֶעֱבִיר יִשְׂרָאֵל בְּתוֹכוֹ כִּי לְעוֹלָם חַסְדּוֹ.
וְנִעֵר פַּרְעֹה וְחֵילוֹ בְיַם סוּף כִּי לְעוֹלָם חַסְדּוֹ.
לְמוֹלִיךְ עַמּוֹ בַּמִּדְבָּר כִּי לְעוֹלָם חַסְדּוֹ.
לְמַכֵּה מְלָכִים גְּדֹלִים כִּי לְעוֹלָם חַסְדּוֹ.
וַיַּהֲרֹג מְלָכִים אַדִּירִים כִּי לְעוֹלָם חַסְדּוֹ.
לְסִיחוֹן מֶלֶךְ הָאֱמֹרִי כִּי לְעוֹלָם חַסְדּוֹ.
וּלְעוֹג מֶלֶךְ הַבָּשָׁן כִּי לְעוֹלָם חַסְדּוֹ.
וְנָתַן אַרְצָם לְנַחֲלָה כִּי לְעוֹלָם חַסְדּוֹ.
נַחֲלָה לְיִשְׂרָאֵל עַבְדּוֹ כִּי לְעוֹלָם חַסְדּוֹ.
שֶׁבְּשִׁפְלֵנוּ זָכַר לָנוּ כִּי לְעוֹלָם חַסְדּוֹ.
וַיִּפְרְקֵנוּ מִצָּרֵינוּ כִּי לְעוֹלָם חַסְדּוֹ.
נֹתֵן לֶחֶם לְכָל בָּשָׂר כִּי לְעוֹלָם חַסְדּוֹ.
הוֹדוּ לְאֵל הַשָּׁמַיִם כִּי לְעוֹלָם חַסְדּוֹ.

Give thanks to the God of Gods
for His kindness is everlasting;

Give thanks to Hashem of Lords	for His ...
Who alone does great wonders	for His ...
Who made the heavens with understanding	for His ...
Who stretched out the earth above the waters	for His ...
Who made the great lights	for His ...
The sun, to rule by day	for His ...
The moon and stars, to rule by night	for His ...
Who struck Egypt through their first-born	for His ...
And brought Israel out of their midst	for His ...
With a strong hand and with an outstretched arm	for His ...
Who split the Sea of Reeds into sections	for His ...
And led Israel through it	for His ...
And cast Pharaoh and his army into the Sea of Reeds	for His ...
Who led His people through the desert	for His ...
Who struck great kings	for His ...
And slew mighty kings	for His ...
Sichon, king of the Amorites	for His ...
And Og, king of Bashan	for His ...
And gave their land as a heritage	for His ...
A heritage to Israel, His servant	for His ...
Who remembered us in our lowliness	for His ...
And delivered us from our oppressors	for His ...
Who gives food to all flesh	for His ...
Thank Hashem of heaven	for His ...

נִשְׁמַת כָּל חַי תְּבָרֵךְ אֶת שִׁמְךָ, יְיָ אֱלֹהֵינוּ, וְרוּחַ כָּל בָּשָׂר תְּפָאֵר וּתְרוֹמֵם זִכְרְךָ, מַלְכֵּנוּ, תָּמִיד. מִן הָעוֹלָם וְעַד הָעוֹלָם אַתָּה אֵל, וּמִבַּלְעָדֶיךָ אֵין לָנוּ מֶלֶךְ גּוֹאֵל וּמוֹשִׁיעַ, פּוֹדֶה וּמַצִּיל וּמְפַרְנֵס וְעוֹנֶה וּמְרַחֵם בְּכָל עֵת צָרָה וְצוּקָה. אֵין לָנוּ מֶלֶךְ עוֹזֵר וְסוֹמֵךְ אֶלָּא אָתָּה. אֱלֹהֵי הָרִאשׁוֹנִים וְהָאַחֲרוֹנִים, אֱלֽוֹהַּ כָּל בְּרִיּוֹת, אֲדוֹן כָּל תּוֹלָדוֹת, הַמְהֻלָּל בְּרֹב הַתִּשְׁבָּחוֹת, הַמְנַהֵג עוֹלָמוֹ בְּחֶסֶד וּבְרִיּוֹתָיו בְּרַחֲמִים. וַייָ עֵר הִנֵּה לֹא יָנוּם וְלֹא יִישָׁן הַמְעוֹרֵר יְשֵׁנִים וְהַמֵּקִיץ נִרְדָּמִים, וְהַמֵּשִׂיחַ אִלְּמִים וְהַמַּתִּיר אֲסוּרִים וְהַסּוֹמֵךְ נוֹפְלִים וְהַזּוֹקֵף כְּפוּפִים וְהַמְפַעֲנֵחַ נֶעֱלָמִים. וּלְךָ לְבַדְּךָ אֲנַחְנוּ מוֹדִים.

וְאִלּוּ פִינוּ מָלֵא שִׁירָה כַּיָּם,
וּלְשׁוֹנֵנוּ רִנָּה כַּהֲמוֹן גַּלָּיו,
וְשִׂפְתוֹתֵינוּ שֶׁבַח כְּמֶרְחֲבֵי רָקִיעַ,
וְעֵינֵינוּ מְאִירוֹת כַּשֶּׁמֶשׁ וְכַיָּרֵחַ, וְיָדֵינוּ פְרוּשׂוֹת כְּנִשְׁרֵי שָׁמַיִם, וְרַגְלֵינוּ קַלּוֹת כָּאַיָּלוֹת אֵין אֲנַחְנוּ מַסְפִּיקִים לְהוֹדוֹת לְךָ, יְיָ אֱלֹהֵינוּ וֵאלֹהֵי אֲבוֹתֵינוּ, וּלְבָרֵךְ אֶת שִׁמְךָ מַלְכֵּנוּ עַל אַחַת, מֵאֶלֶף, אַלְפֵי אֲלָפִים וְרִבֵּי רְבָבוֹת פְּעָמִים, הַטּוֹבוֹת שֶׁעָשִׂיתָ עִם אֲבוֹתֵינוּ וְעִמָּנוּ. מִמִּצְרַיִם גְּאַלְתָּנוּ, יְיָ אֱלֹהֵינוּ, וּמִבֵּית עֲבָדִים פְּדִיתָנוּ, בְּרָעָב זַנְתָּנוּ וּבְשָׂבָע כִּלְכַּלְתָּנוּ, מֵחֶרֶב הִצַּלְתָּנוּ וּמִדֶּבֶר מִלַּטְתָּנוּ, וּמֵחֳלָיִם רָעִים וְרַבִּים וְנֶאֱמָנִים דִּלִּיתָנוּ. עַד הֵנָּה עֲזָרוּנוּ רַחֲמֶיךָ וְלֹא עֲזָבוּנוּ חֲסָדֶיךָ, וְאַל תִּטְּשֵׁנוּ, יְיָ אֱלֹהֵינוּ, לָנֶצַח.

The soul of every living being shall bless Your Name, Hashem, our God; and the spirit of all flesh shall always glorify and exalt Your remembrance, our King. From the beginning to the end of the world You are Almighty God; and other than You we have no King, Redeemer and Savior who delivers, rescues, sustains, answers and is merciful in every time of trouble and distress; we have no King but You. [You are] Hashem of the first and of the last [generations], Hashem of all creatures, God of all events, who is extolled with manifold praises, who directs His world with kindness and His creatures with compassion. Behold, Hashem neither slumbers nor sleeps. He arouses the sleepers and awakens the slumberous, gives speech to the mute, releases the bound, supports the falling and raises up those who are bowed. To You alone we give thanks.

Even if our mouths were filled with song as the sea, and our tongues with joyous singing like the multitudes of its waves, and our lips with praise like the expanse of the sky; and our eyes shining like the sun and the moon, and our hands spread out like the eagles of heaven, and our feet swift like deer we would still be unable to thank You Hashem, our God and God of our fathers, and to bless Your Name, for even one of the thousands of millions, and myriads of myriads, of favors, miracles and wonders which You have done for us and for our fathers before us. Hashem, our God. You have redeemed us from Egypt, You have freed us from the house of bondage, You have fed us in famine and nourished us in plenty; You have saved us from the sword and delivered us from pestilence, and raised us from evil and lasting maladies. Until now Your mercies have helped us, and Your kindnesses have not forsaken us; and do not abandon us, Hashem our God, forever!

עַל כֵּן אֵבָרִים שֶׁפִּלַּגְתָּ בָּנוּ וְרוּחַ וּנְשָׁמָה שֶׁנָּפַחְתָּ בְּאַפֵּינוּ וְלָשׁוֹן אֲשֶׁר שַׂמְתָּ בְּפִינוּ הֵן הֵם יוֹדוּ וִיבָרְכוּ וִישַׁבְּחוּ וִיפָאֲרוּ וִירוֹמְמוּ וְיַעֲרִיצוּ וְיַקְדִּישׁוּ וְיַמְלִיכוּ אֶת שִׁמְךָ מַלְכֵּנוּ. כִּי כָל פֶּה לְךָ יוֹדֶה, וְכָל לָשׁוֹן לְךָ תִשָּׁבַע, וְכָל בֶּרֶךְ לְךָ תִכְרַע, וְכָל קוֹמָה לְפָנֶיךָ תִשְׁתַּחֲוֶה, וְכָל לְבָבוֹת יִירָאוּךָ, וְכָל קֶרֶב וּכְלָיוֹת יְזַמְּרוּ לִשְׁמֶךָ, כַּדָּבָר שֶׁכָּתוּב, כָּל עַצְמוֹתַי תֹּאמַרְנָה: יְיָ, מִי כָמוֹךָ מַצִּיל עָנִי מֵחָזָק מִמֶּנּוּ וְעָנִי וְאֶבְיוֹן מִגֹּזְלוֹ. מִי יִדְמֶה לָּךְ וּמִי יִשְׁוֶה לָּךְ וּמִי יַעֲרָךְ לָךְ הָאֵל הַגָּדוֹל, הַגִּבּוֹר וְהַנּוֹרָא, אֵל עֶלְיוֹן, קוֹנֵה שָׁמַיִם וָאָרֶץ. נְהַלֶּלְךָ וּנְשַׁבֵּחֲךָ וּנְפָאֶרְךָ וּנְבָרֵךְ אֶת שֵׁם קָדְשֶׁךָ, כָּאָמוּר: לְדָוִד, בָּרְכִי נַפְשִׁי אֶת יְיָ וְכָל קְרָבַי אֶת שֵׁם קָדְשׁוֹ.

הָאֵל בְּתַעֲצֻמוֹת עֻזֶּךָ, הַגָּדוֹל בִּכְבוֹד שְׁמֶךָ, הַגִּבּוֹר לָנֶצַח וְהַנּוֹרָא בְּנוֹרְאוֹתֶיךָ, הַמֶּלֶךְ הַיּוֹשֵׁב עַל כִּסֵּא רָם וְנִשָּׂא.

שׁוֹכֵן עַד מָרוֹם וְקָדוֹשׁ שְׁמוֹ. וְכָתוּב:
רַנְּנוּ צַדִּיקִים בַּיהוה, לַיְשָׁרִים נָאוָה תְהִלָּה.
בְּפִי יְשָׁרִים תִּתְהַלָּל
וּבְדִבְרֵי צַדִּיקִים תִּתְבָּרַךְ
וּבִלְשׁוֹן חֲסִידִים תִּתְרוֹמָם
וּבְקֶרֶב קְדוֹשִׁים תִּתְקַדָּשׁ.

וּבְמַקְהֲלוֹת רִבְבוֹת עַמְּךָ בֵּית יִשְׂרָאֵל בְּרִנָּה יִתְפָּאֵר שִׁמְךָ, מַלְכֵּנוּ, בְּכָל דּוֹר וָדוֹר, שֶׁכֵּן חוֹבַת כָּל הַיְצוּרִים לְפָנֶיךָ, יְיָ אֱלֹהֵינוּ וֵאלֹהֵי אֲבוֹתֵינוּ, לְהוֹדוֹת לְהַלֵּל לְשַׁבֵּחַ, לְפָאֵר

Therefore, the limbs which You have arranged within us, and the spirit and soul which You have breathed into our nostrils, and the tongue which You have placed in our mouth they all shall thank, bless, praise, glorify, exalt, adore, sanctify and proclaim the sovereignty of Your Name, our King. For every mouth shall offer thanks to You, every tongue shall swear by You, every eye shall look to You, every knee shall bend to You, all who stand erect shall, l bow down before You, all hearts shall fear You, and every innermost part shall sing praise to Your Name, as it is written: "All my bones will say, Hashem, who is like You; You save the poor from one stronger than he, the poor and the needy from one who would rob him!" Who can be likened to You, who is equal to You, who can be compared to You, the great, mighty, awesome God, God most high, Possessor of heaven and earth! We will laud You, praise You and glorify You, and we will bless Your holy Name, as it is said: " by David; bless Hashem, O my soul, and all that is within me [bless] His holy Name."

You are the Almighty God in the power of Your strength; the Great in the glory of Your Name; the Mighty forever, and the Awesome in Your awesome deeds; the King who sits upon a lofty and exalted throne.

He who dwells for eternity, lofty and holy is His Name. And it is written: "Sing joyously to Hashem, you righteous; it befits the upright to offer praise." By the mouth of the upright You are exalted; by the lips of the righteous You are blessed; by the tongue of the pious You are sanctified; and among the holy ones You are praised.

In the assemblies of the myriads of Your people, the House of Israel, Your Name, our King, shall be glorified with song in every generation. For such is the obligation of all creatures before You, Hashem, our God and God of our fathers, to thank, to laud, to

לְרוֹמֵם לְהַדֵּר לְבָרֵךְ, לְעַלֵּה וּלְקַלֵּס עַל כָּל דִּבְרֵי שִׁירוֹת
וְתִשְׁבְּחוֹת דָּוִד בֶּן יִשַׁי עַבְדְּךָ, מְשִׁיחֶךָ.

וּבְכֵן יִשְׁתַּבַּח שִׁמְךָ לָעַד מַלְכֵּנוּ,
הָאֵל הַמֶּלֶךְ הַגָּדוֹל וְהַקָּדוֹשׁ בַּשָּׁמַיִם וּבָאָרֶץ,
כִּי לְךָ נָאֶה, יְיָ אֱלֹהֵינוּ וֵאלֹהֵי אֲבוֹתֵינוּ,
שִׁיר וּשְׁבָחָה, הַלֵּל וְזִמְרָה, עֹז וּמֶמְשָׁלָה,
נֶצַח, גְּדֻלָּה וּגְבוּרָה, תְּהִלָּה וְתִפְאֶרֶת, קְדֻשָּׁה וּמַלְכוּת.
בְּרָכוֹת וְהוֹדָאוֹת מֵעַתָּה וְעַד עוֹלָם.
בָּרוּךְ אַתָּה יְיָ, אֵל מֶלֶךְ גָּדוֹל בַּתִּשְׁבָּחוֹת,
אֵל הַהוֹדָאוֹת, אֲדוֹן הַנִּפְלָאוֹת, הַבּוֹחֵר בְּשִׁירֵי זִמְרָה,
מֶלֶךְ אֵל חֵי הָעוֹלָמִים.

כוס רביעית

הִנְנִי מוּכָן וּמְזֻמָּן לְקַיֵּם מִצְוַת כּוֹס רְבִיעִי שֶׁהוּא כְּנֶגֶד בְּשׂוֹרַת הַיְשׁוּעָה, שֶׁאָמַר הַקָּדוֹשׁ בָּרוּךְ הוּא לְיִשְׂרָאֵל "וְלָקַחְתִּי אֶתְכֶם לִי לְעָם וְהָיִיתִי לָכֶם לֵאלֹהִים".

בָּרוּךְ אַתָּה יְיָ אֱלֹהֵינוּ מֶלֶךְ הָעוֹלָם בּוֹרֵא פְּרִי הַגָּפֶן.

וְשׁוֹתֶה בַּהֲסָבַת שְׂמֹאל

בָּרוּךְ אַתָּה יְיָ אֱלֹהֵינוּ מֶלֶךְ הָעוֹלָם, עַל הַגֶּפֶן וְעַל פְּרִי הַגֶּפֶן, עַל תְּנוּבַת הַשָּׂדֶה וְעַל אֶרֶץ חֶמְדָּה טוֹבָה וּרְחָבָה שֶׁרָצִיתָ וְהִנְחַלְתָּ לַאֲבוֹתֵינוּ לֶאֱכֹל מִפִּרְיָהּ וְלִשְׂבֹּעַ מִטּוּבָהּ רַחֵם נָא יְיָ אֱלֹקֵינוּ עַל יִשְׂרָאֵל עַמֶּךָ

praise, to glorify, to exalt, to adore, to bless, to elevate and to honor You, even beyond all the words of songs and praises of David son of Yishai, Your anointed servant.

And therefore may Your Name be praised forever, our King, the great and holy God and King in heaven and on earth. For to You, Hashem, our God and God of our fathers, forever befits song and praise, laud and hymn, strength and dominion, victory, greatness and might, glory, splendor, holiness and sovereignty; blessings and thanksgivings to Your great and holy Name; from the beginning to the end of the world You are Almighty God. Blessed are You, Hashem, Almighty God, King, great and extolled in praises, God of thanksgivings, Hashem of wonders, Creator of all souls, Master of all creatures, who takes pleasure in songs of praise; the only King, the Life of all worlds.

The Fourth Cup

Blessed are You, Hashem, our God, King of the universe, **who creates the fruit of the vine**.

Drink in reclining position.

Concluding Blessing for the Wine:

Blessed are You, Hashem our God, King of the universe for the vine and the fruit of the vine, for the produce of the field, and for the precious, good and spacious land which You have favored to give as an heritage to our fathers, to eat of its fruit and

וְעַל יְרוּשָׁלַיִם עִירֶךָ וְעַל צִיּוֹן מִשְׁכַּן כְּבוֹדֶךָ וְעַל מִזְבְּחֶךָ וְעַל הֵיכָלֶךָ וּבְנֵה יְרוּשָׁלַיִם עִיר הַקֹּדֶשׁ בִּמְהֵרָה בְיָמֵינוּ וְהַעֲלֵנוּ לְתוֹכָהּ וְשַׂמְּחֵנוּ בְּבִנְיָנָהּ וְנֹאכַל מִפִּרְיָהּ וְנִשְׂבַּע מִטּוּבָהּ וּנְבָרֶכְךָ עָלֶיהָ בִּקְדֻשָּׁה וּבְטָהֳרָה (בְּשַׁבָּת: וּרְצֵה וְהַחֲלִיצֵנוּ בְּיוֹם הַשַּׁבָּת הַזֶּה) וְשַׂמְּחֵנוּ בְּיוֹם חַג הַמַּצּוֹת הַזֶּה, כִּי אַתָּה יְיָ טוֹב וּמֵטִיב לַכֹּל וְנוֹדֶה לְּךָ עַל הָאָרֶץ וְעַל פְּרִי הַגָּפֶן. בָּרוּךְ אַתָּה יְיָ עַל הָאָרֶץ וְעַל פְּרִי הַגָּפֶן. (עַל יַיִן וּמִיץ עֲנָבִים מִתּוֹצֶרֶת הָאָרֶץ מְסַיֵּם: כִּי אַתָּה יְיָ טוֹב וּמֵטִיב לַכֹּל וְנוֹדֶה לְּךָ עַל הָאָרֶץ וְעַל פְּרִי גַפְנָהּ. בָּרוּךְ אַתָּה יְיָ עַל הָאָרֶץ וְעַל פְּרִי גַפְנָהּ.)

Passover – A Time for Reflection and Change

Rosh Hashanah and Pesach represent the two polar opposites within the divine attributes. The *Zohar* (3:309a) says, "One pushes away with the left hand and draws near with the right hand – this is Rosh Hashanah and Pesach." Pesach is the right hand of God, which brings about repentance through love, while *Rosh Hashanah* is the left hand, which inspires repentance through firmness and judgment.

Rabbi Jerachmiel Danziger

The laws of Yom Kippur are constructed in such a way that a person is forced to focus on himself or herself rather than others. The prohibitions, based on the obligation to "afflict ourselves," create a solitary experience. Fasting precludes the social activity of meals; the prohibition to bathe and put on perfume encourages a physical distance between husband and wife, be satiated by its goodness. Have mercy, Hashem our God, on Israel Your people, on Jerusalem Your city, on Zion the abode of Your glory, on Your altar and on Your Temple. Rebuild Jerusalem, the holy city, speedily in our days, and bring us up into it, and make us rejoice in it, and we will bless You in holiness and purity (On Shabbat add: May it please You to strengthen us on this Shabbat day) and remember us for good on this day of the Festival of Matzot. For You, Hashem, are good and do good to all, and we thank You for the land and for the fruit of the vine. Blessed are You, Hashem, for the land and for the fruit of the vine.

---

and even friends. Although we acknowledge in the liturgy our responsibility and roles within the community, the onus is on the individual to examine his or her own behavior.

Pesach, in contrast, highlights the creation of a community that joins together for the common good and mutual defense. True, an individual must first reflect on his or her own personal freedom – "Every individual is required to personally feel like he or she left Egypt" – but this awareness is followed by a deep identification with the broader community, culminating with the societal covenant at Mount Sinai.

Yom Kippur emphasizes the individual and personal introspection: a candid evaluation of our actions in the past year, and new resolutions for the coming year. Pesach is also about personal introspection but utilizes community, family and history as a springboard toward personal reflection and change.

Appreciating Others and Being Appreciated

When a friend does something nice for you, the act itself isn't as significant as what it symbolizes. Short of saving your life, you could probably live and function without this kind deed. But the knowledge that you have a friend is priceless and irreplaceable. The feeling of friendship is one you never wish to lose.

When we fail to express gratitude, we are harming ourselves by not recognizing that we have friends. The one who bestowed the favor is hurt because he is not appreciated, but the recipient is hurt even more because he does not even realize that he is loved and cared for.

Gratitude is a prominent theme of the Haggadah: towards our friends, family, and of course, God.

*Paraphrased from the teachings of Rabbi Yochanan Zweig,
Founder and head of the Talmudic University of Florida*

Passover – the Holiday of Transformation

It was written earlier that bread is a transformational food, but on Pesach this normal transformation of wheat to bread is interrupted. It is as if our normal course of obtaining sustenance is paused, and we ask: "How come today is different? We normally eat regular bread but why this cessation of normal food preparation? What message is this pause giving us?"

Perhaps this can be compared to another well-known interruption on Yom Kippur, namely, the blowing of the Shofar. Of course, the prayer services on Yom Kippur are longer and more somber that any other Jewish holiday, but basically the trappings of the synagogue services are not too different from any other major Jewish holiday until the middle of the morning

It's About Continuity

The Jewish people as a whole and collective body always prided themselves on their acute sense of memory. Israel remembered that the Exodus from Egypt occurred on a Thursday, that the revelation on Sinai took place on Shabbat, that Rabbi Akiva was executed by the Romans in the hippodrome of Caesarea on Yom Kippur, and that the Jews of Ethiopia are descended from a "peace corps" mission of members of the tribe of Dan whom Solomon sent out at the request of the Queen of Sheba. With such exacting memory we have also recalled the people who populated the generations of Israel, the great heroes and the despised villains, as well as the historical events of the time.

This sense of memory was based on the obligation of one generation to transmit not only its accumulated knowledge to the next generation, but more importantly, to transmit to future generation the very power of memory itself.

Jewish parents trained Jewish children to remember – to remember the Land of Israel even though they never saw that land, to remember the covenant with God at Sinai even though adherence to that covenant brought with it sacrifice and difficulties, to remember to be good and kind in a world that lacked compassion. In short, to remember to be Jews!

Rabbi Berel Wein

---

service, including parts of the silent portions of the Musaf section, when the normal regimen is interrupted by the sound of a musical instrument – the Shofar. The same questions can be asked on Yom Kippur: How come today is different? Normally we pray without interruption, but not on Yom Kippur. What message is this pause giving us?

It is interesting that the last words in the Yom Kippur machzor/prayer book and the Haggadah are the same: Next year in Jerusalem! Perhaps it is because both Yom Kippur and Pesach are transformational holidays. In Yom Kippur the individual appraises himself as he relates to himself apart from the community. In Pesach the individual appraises himself as he relates to himself and how he relates within his community. Next year in Jerusalem! May we all make aliyah – and be transformed upward.

Israel the Destination

Glory paved her path
History guarded her way;
though reluctant to show itself, Fate
shaped her contours from obscurity.
Providence was already manifest,
preparing for the event.
Israel is primed for the festivities
a happiness beyond compare
now everyone is preparing
to give her the honor she deserves.
For behold:
two thousand years are as nought
and the past fifty,
an eternity.
Your fields bloom
and hills covered with forests
bear tidings of a Spring to come.
Your essence, Israel,
is the dust of crematoria
and your son's blood,
spilt in righteous defense;
these are the laurels
that adorn your head.
Israel, today is the occasion
of your first Jubilee
a sign and a wonder
for all the future.
Today is your day, Israel
and we celebrate
with honor and praise!

Arie Comey

נִרְצָה

חֲסַל סִדּוּר פֶּסַח כְּהִלְכָתוֹ, כְּכָל מִשְׁפָּטוֹ וְחֻקָּתוֹ.
כַּאֲשֶׁר זָכִינוּ לְסַדֵּר אוֹתוֹ כֵּן נִזְכֶּה לַעֲשׂוֹתוֹ.
זָךְ שׁוֹכֵן מְעוֹנָה, קוֹמֵם קְהַל עֲדַת מִי מָנָה.
בְּקָרוֹב נַהֵל נִטְעֵי כַנָּה פְּדוּיִים לְצִיּוֹן בְּרִנָּה.
לְשָׁנָה הַבָּאָה בִּירוּשָׁלָיִם.

לְשָׁנָה הַבָּאָה בִּירוּשָׁלַיִם הַבְּנוּיָה.

Past and Present

And thus we establish, in this, the firstborn of Jewish festivals, the special character of Jewish memory. We are commanded to recall the past, in order to remember the present – to see it clearly, to know it fully, in all its possibilities – in the light of our future redemption. We Jews stand between redemption, as it were, looking back in order to look forward: we thus come to see that we also stand among redemptions – acts of freedom, births of possibility – that we might not have seen, or assisted in, without the paradigm of Pesach. Messianic hope would not be credible in the world, as we know it were it not for the fact – rehearsed at Pesach – that redemption has occurred. Because it has, because the events of liberation that we recall are as real as acts of cruelty or arbitrariness of which we need no reminder, we are made bold enough to hope for the Messiah. And that reservoir of faith, the gift of memory, makes all the difference as we go about the business of living in the world, and trying to redeem it.

Arnold Eisen

Nirtzah

The order of the Pesach service is now completed with its laws, ordinances and statutes. Just as we were privileged to arrange it, so may we merit to perform it. O Pure One, Who dwells on high, raise up the congregation which is without number. Soon guide the offshoots of Your plants, redeemed to Zion rejoicing in song.

NEXT YEAR IN JERUSALEM!

יֵשׁ נוֹהֲגִין בְּחוּץ לָאָרֶץ בְּלֵיל שֵׁנִי שֶׁל פֶּסַח לִסְפֹּר כַּאן סְפִירַת הָעֹמֶר:

בָּרוּךְ אַתָּה יְיָ אֱלֹהֵינוּ מֶלֶךְ הָעוֹלָם, אֲשֶׁר קִדְּשָׁנוּ בְּמִצְווֹתָיו וְצִוָּנוּ עַל סְפִירַת הָעֹמֶר.
הַיּוֹם יוֹם אֶחָד בָּעֹמֶר.

בְּלֵיל רִאשׁוֹן אוֹמְרִים:

וּבְכֵן וַיְהִי בַּחֲצִי הַלַּיְלָה

אָז רוֹב נִסִּים הִפְלֵאתָ בַּלַּיְלָה,
בְּרֹאשׁ אַשְׁמוֹרֶת זֶה הַלַּיְלָה,
גֵּר צֶדֶק נִצַּחְתּוֹ כְּנֶחֱלַק לוֹ לַיְלָה,
וַיְהִי בַּחֲצִי הַלַּיְלָה.

דַּנְתָּ מֶלֶךְ גְּרָר בַּחֲלוֹם הַלַּיְלָה,
הִפְחַדְתָּ אֲרַמִּי בְּאֶמֶשׁ לַיְלָה,
וַיָּשַׂר יִשְׂרָאֵל לְמַלְאָךְ וַיּוּכַל לוֹ לַיְלָה,
וַיְהִי בַּחֲצִי הַלַּיְלָה.

זֶרַע בְּכוֹרֵי פַתְרוֹס מָחַצְתָּ בַּחֲצִי הַלַּיְלָה,
חֵילָם לֹא מָצְאוּ בְּקוּמָם בַּלַּיְלָה,
טִיסַת נְגִיד חֲרֹשֶׁת סִלִּיתָ בְּכוֹכְבֵי לַיְלָה,
וַיְהִי בַּחֲצִי הַלַּיְלָה.

Outside of the land of Israel during the second night of Passover one begins the counting of the Omer:

Blessed are You, Hashem, our God, King of the Universe, Who has sanctified us with His commandments, and has commanded us concerning counting of the Omer: Today is one day of the Omer.

On the first night of Passover, recite:

And it came to pass, at midnight

You made miracles, at night
When watchers blink to see through night.
Abraham conquered four kings by night,
And it came to pass, at midnight

You blighted Gerar in a dream by night,
You warned Laban on the night
Before. Israel wrestled with an angel all night.
And it came to pass, at midnight

You crushed Egypt's first-born seed. The night-
Mare of a loaf of bread doomed Midian one night.
You cut down Sisera's armies under starry night.
And it came to pass, at midnight

יָעַץ מְחָרֵף לְנוֹפֵף אִוּוּי הוֹבַשְׁתָּ פְּגָרָיו בַּלַּיְלָה,
כָּרַע בֵּל וּמַצָּבוֹ בְּאִישׁוֹן לַיְלָה,
לְאִישׁ חֲמוּדוֹת נִגְלָה רָז חֲזוֹת לַיְלָה,
וַיְהִי בַּחֲצִי הַלַּיְלָה.

מִשְׁתַּכֵּר בִּכְלֵי קֹדֶשׁ נֶהֱרַג בּוֹ בַּלַּיְלָה,
נוֹשַׁע מִבּוֹר אֲרָיוֹת פּוֹתֵר בִּעֲתוּתֵי לַיְלָה,
שִׂנְאָה נָטַר אֲגָגִי וְכָתַב סְפָרִים בַּלַּיְלָה,
וַיְהִי בַּחֲצִי הַלַּיְלָה.

עוֹרַרְתָּ נִצְחֲךָ עָלָיו בְּנֶדֶד שְׁנַת לַיְלָה,
פּוּרָה תִדְרוֹךְ לְשׁוֹמֵר מַה מִּלַּיְלָה,
צָרַח כַּשּׁוֹמֵר וְשָׂח אָתָא בֹקֶר וְגַם לַיְלָה,
וַיְהִי בַּחֲצִי הַלַּיְלָה.

קָרֵב יוֹם אֲשֶׁר הוּא לֹא יוֹם וְלֹא לַיְלָה,
רָם הוֹדַע כִּי לְךָ הַיּוֹם אַף לְךָ הַלַּיְלָה,
שׁוֹמְרִים הַפְקֵד לְעִירְךָ כָּל הַיּוֹם וְכָל הַלַּיְלָה,
תָּאִיר כְּאוֹר יוֹם חֶשְׁכַת לַיְלָה,
וַיְהִי בַּחֲצִי הַלַּיְלָה.

You turned the taunter's army into a corpses' camp. Overnight
The dragon Bel fell from his pedestal, while in the night
Daniel dreamed mysteries of coming night.
And it came to pass, at midnight

Belshazzar perished in God's cups that night.
Daniel, reader of the words, stayed with lions for a night.
Haman the hater wrote his letters late at night.
And it came to pass, at midnight

You toppled Haman during Ahasuerus' sleepless night.
You tread the winepress; asked, "What of the night?"
You answer, "The day cometh, and also the night,"
And it came to pass, at midnight

Bring quickly, Lord, the day which is not day or night.
The day is yours, God, and so is the night.
Set guards about your city day and night,
Give us vision clear by day by night,
And it came to pass, at midnight

בְּלֵיל שֵׁנִי אוֹמְרִים:

וּבְכֵן וַאֲמַרְתֶּם זֶבַח פֶּסַח

אֹמֶץ גְּבוּרוֹתֶיךָ הִפְלֵאתָ בַּפֶּסַח, **בְּ**רֹאשׁ כָּל מוֹעֲדוֹת נִשֵּׂאתָ פֶּסַח, **גִּ**לִּיתָ לְאֶזְרָחִי חֲצוֹת לֵיל פֶּסַח, **וַאֲמַרְתֶּם זֶבַח פֶּסַח**. **דְּ**לָתָיו דָּפַקְתָּ כְּחֹם הַיּוֹם בַּפֶּסַח, **הִ**סְעִיד נוֹצְצִים עֻגוֹת מַצּוֹת בַּפֶּסַח, **וְ**אֶל הַבָּקָר רָץ זֵכֶר לְשׁוֹר עֵרֶךְ פֶּסַח, **וַאֲמַרְתֶּם זֶבַח פֶּסַח**. **ז**וֹעֲמוּ סְדוֹמִים וְלוֹהֲטוּ בָּאֵשׁ בַּפֶּסַח, **חֻ**לַּץ לוֹט מֵהֶם וּמַצּוֹת אָפָה בְּקֵץ פֶּסַח, **טִ**אטֵאתָ אַדְמַת מֹף וְנֹף בְּעָבְרְךָ בַּפֶּסַח, **וַאֲמַרְתֶּם זֶבַח פֶּסַח**. **יָ**הּ רֹאשׁ כָּל אוֹן מָחַצְתָּ בְּלֵיל שִׁמּוּר פֶּסַח, **כַּ**בִּיר, עַל בֵּן בְּכוֹר פָּסַחְתָּ בְּדַם פֶּסַח, **לְ**בִלְתִּי תֵּת מַשְׁחִית לָבֹא בִפְתָחַי בַּפֶּסַח, **וַאֲמַרְתֶּם זֶבַח פֶּסַח**. **מְ**סֻגֶּרֶת סֻגָּרָה בְּעִתּוֹתֵי פֶּסַח, **נִ**שְׁמְדָה מִדְיָן בִּצְלִיל שְׂעוֹרֵי עֹמֶר פֶּסַח, **שׂ**וֹרְפוּ מִשְׁמַנֵּי פּוּל וְלוּד בִּיקַד יְקוֹד פֶּסַח, **וַאֲמַרְתֶּם זֶבַח פֶּסַח**. **עוֹ**ד הַיּוֹם בְּנֹב לַעֲמוֹד עַד גָּעָה עוֹנַת פֶּסַח, **פַּ**ס יַד כָּתְבָה לְקַעֲקֵעַ צוּל בַּפֶּסַח, **צָ**פֹה הַצָּפִית עָרוֹךְ הַשֻּׁלְחָן בַּפֶּסַח, **וַאֲמַרְתֶּם זֶבַח פֶּסַח**. **קָ**הָל כִּנְּסָה הֲדַסָּה לְשַׁלֵּשׁ צוֹם בַּפֶּסַח, **רֹ**אשׁ מִבֵּית רָשָׁע מָחַצְתָּ בְּעֵץ חֲמִשִּׁים בַּפֶּסַח, **שְׁ**תֵּי אֵלֶּה רֶגַע תָּבִיא לְעוּצִית בַּפֶּסַח, **תָּ**עֹז יָדְךָ וְתָרוּם יְמִינְךָ כְּלֵיל הִתְקַדֵּשׁ חַג פֶּסַח, **וַאֲמַרְתֶּם זֶבַח פֶּסַח.**

On the second night of Passover, recite:

And you shall say: "It is the sacrifice of the Lord's Passover."

You showed your power on Passover. As our first festival you made the Passover. You visited with Abraham on Passover. **And you shall say: "It is the sacrifice of the Lord's Passover."** You rapped upon his tent flap in the heat of day, on Passover. He served your messengers unleavened bread on Passover. And sacrificed a tender calf for Passover. **And you shall say: "It is the sacrifice of the Lord's Passover."** Sodom was consumed by fire on Passover. But Lot, spared, baked unleavened bread for Passover. You desolated Egypt on the Passover. **And you shall say: "It is the sacrifice of the Lord's Passover."** Egypt's first-born you destroyed that Passover. Death passed us over, passed our doors, that Passover. No evil came to Israel on Passover. **And you shall say: "It is the sacrifice of the Lord's Passover."** Jericho's walls tumbled after Passover. Gideon dreamed of Midian's fall at Passover. The Assyrians were consumed by flames on Passover. **And you shall say: "It is the sacrifice of the Lord's Passover."** Sennacherib would still be at Nob, if not for Passover. The handwriting on the wall was read at Passover. While Belsahazzar's feast was set on Passover. **And you shall say: "It is the sacrifice of the Lord's Passover."** Queen Esther called a three-day fast on Passover. And Haman hung from the gallows tree on Passover. Those who hate us will be punished twice on Passover. By your right arm, then as in Egypt on the Passover. **And you shall say: "It is the sacrifice of the Lord's Passover."**

כִּי לוֹ נָאֶה, כִּי לוֹ יָאֶה [כֶּתֶר מְלוּכָה].

אַדִּיר בִּמְלוּכָה, **בָּ**חוּר כַּהֲלָכָה, **גְּ**דוּדָיו יֹאמְרוּ לוֹ: לְךָ וּלְךָ,
לְךָ כִּי לְךָ, לְךָ אַף לְךָ, לְךָ יְיָ הַמַּמְלָכָה,
כִּי לוֹ נָאֶה, כִּי לוֹ יָאֶה [כֶּתֶר מְלוּכָה].

דָּגוּל בִּמְלוּכָה, **הָ**דוּר כַּהֲלָכָה, **וָ**תִיקָיו יֹאמְרוּ לוֹ: לְךָ וּלְךָ,
לְךָ כִּי לְךָ, לְךָ אַף לְךָ, לְךָ יְיָ הַמַּמְלָכָה,
כִּי לוֹ נָאֶה, כִּי לוֹ יָאֶה [כֶּתֶר מְלוּכָה].

זַכַּאי בִּמְלוּכָה, **חָ**סִין כַּהֲלָכָה **ט**ַפְסְרָיו יֹאמְרוּ לוֹ: לְךָ וּלְךָ,
לְךָ כִּי לְךָ, לְךָ אַף לְךָ, לְךָ יְיָ הַמַּמְלָכָה,
כִּי לוֹ נָאֶה, כִּי לוֹ יָאֶה [כֶּתֶר מְלוּכָה].

יָחִיד בִּמְלוּכָה, **כַּ**בִּיר כַּהֲלָכָה **לִ**מּוּדָיו יֹאמְרוּ לוֹ: לְךָ וּלְךָ, לְךָ
כִּי לְךָ, לְךָ אַף לְךָ, לְךָ יְיָ הַמַּמְלָכָה,
כִּי לוֹ נָאֶה, כִּי לוֹ יָאֶה [כֶּתֶר מְלוּכָה].

מוֹשֵׁל בִּמְלוּכָה, **נ**וֹרָא כַּהֲלָכָה **ס**ְבִיבָיו יֹאמְרוּ לוֹ: לְךָ וּלְךָ,
לְךָ כִּי לְךָ, לְךָ אַף לְךָ, לְךָ יְיָ הַמַּמְלָכָה,
כִּי לוֹ נָאֶה, כִּי לוֹ יָאֶה [כֶּתֶר מְלוּכָה].

עָנָיו בִּמְלוּכָה, **פּ**וֹדֶה כַּהֲלָכָה, **צַ**דִּיקָיו יֹאמְרוּ לוֹ: לְךָ וּלְךָ,
לְךָ כִּי לְךָ, לְךָ אַף לְךָ, לְךָ יְיָ הַמַּמְלָכָה,
כִּי לוֹ נָאֶה, כִּי לוֹ יָאֶה [כֶּתֶר מְלוּכָה].

To Him praise is due!
To Him praise is fitting!

Powerful in kingship, perfectly distinguished, His companies of angels say to Him: Yours and only Yours: Yours, yes Yours; Yours, surely Yours; Yours, Hashem, is the sovereignty.
To Him praise is due! To Him praise is fitting!

Supreme in kingship, perfectly glorious, His faithful say to Him: Yours and only Yours: Yours, yes Yours; Yours, surely Yours; Yours, Hashem, is the sovereignty.
To Him praise is due! To Him praise is fitting!

Pure in kingship, perfectly mighty, His angels say to Him: Yours and only Yours: Yours, yes Yours; Yours, surely Yours; Yours, Hashem, is the sovereignty.
To Him praise is due! To Him praise is fitting!

Alone in kingship, perfectly omnipotent, His scholars say to Him: Yours and only Yours: Yours, yes Yours; Yours, surely Yours; Yours, Hashem, is the sovereignty.
To Him praise is due! To Him praise is fitting!

Commanding in kingship, perfectly wondrous, His surrounding (angels) say to Him: Yours and only Yours: Yours, yes Yours; Yours, surely Yours; Yours, Hashem, is the sovereignty.
To Him praise is due! To Him praise is fitting!

Gentle in kingship, perfectly the Redeemer, his righteous say to Him: Yours and only Yours: Yours, yes Yours; Yours, surely Yours; Yours, Hashem, is the sovereignty.
To Him praise is due! To Him praise is fitting!

קָדוֹשׁ בִּמְלוּכָה, רַחוּם כַּהֲלָכָה שִׁנְאַנָּיו יֹאמְרוּ לוֹ: לְךָ וּלְךָ,
לְךָ כִּי לְךָ, לְךָ אַף לְךָ, לְךָ יְיָ הַמַּמְלָכָה,
כִּי לוֹ נָאֶה, כִּי לוֹ יָאֶה [כֶּתֶר מְלוּכָה].

תַּקִּיף בִּמְלוּכָה, תּוֹמֵךְ כַּהֲלָכָה תְּמִימָיו יֹאמְרוּ לוֹ: לְךָ וּלְךָ,
לְךָ כִּי לְךָ, לְךָ אַף לְךָ, לְךָ יְיָ הַמַּמְלָכָה,
כִּי לוֹ נָאֶה, כִּי לוֹ יָאֶה [כֶּתֶר מְלוּכָה].

אַדִּיר הוּא יִבְנֶה בֵּיתוֹ בְּקָרוֹב.

בִּמְהֵרָה, בִּמְהֵרָה, בְּיָמֵינוּ בְּקָרוֹב.
אֵל בְּנֵה, אֵל בְּנֵה, בְּנֵה בֵּיתְךָ בְּקָרוֹב.

בָּחוּר הוּא, גָּדוֹל הוּא, דָּגוּל הוּא יִבְנֶה בֵּיתוֹ בְּקָרוֹב.
בִּמְהֵרָה, בִּמְהֵרָה, בְּיָמֵינוּ בְּקָרוֹב.
אֵל בְּנֵה, אֵל בְּנֵה, בְּנֵה בֵּיתְךָ בְּקָרוֹב.

הָדוּר הוּא, וָתִיק הוּא, זַכַּאי הוּא,
חָסִיד הוּא יִבְנֶה בֵּיתוֹ בְּקָרוֹב.
בִּמְהֵרָה, בִּמְהֵרָה, בְּיָמֵינוּ בְּקָרוֹב.
בִּמְהֵרָה, בִּמְהֵרָה, בְּיָמֵינוּ בְּקָרוֹב.

Holy in kingship, perfectly merciful, His troops of angels say to Him: Yours and only Yours: Yours, yes Yours; Yours, surely Yours; Yours, Hashem, is the sovereignty.
To Him praise is due! To Him praise is fitting!

Almighty in kingship, perfectly sustaining, His perfect ones say to Him: Yours and only Yours: Yours, yes Yours; Yours, surely Yours; Yours, Hashem, is the sovereignty.
To Him praise is due! To Him praise is fitting!

Adir Hu

God is strong, God will build the Temple soon:
Quickly, while we're living, soon. Build the Temple soon.

God alone, stark and strong, God will build the Temple soon:
Quickly, while we're living, soon.
Build the Temple soon.

God of light, out of time, God will build the Temple soon:
Quickly, while we're living, soon.
Build the Temple soon.

טָהוֹר הוּא, יָחִיד הוּא, כַּבִּיר הוּא,
לָמוּד הוּא, מֶלֶךְ הוּא יִבְנֶה בֵּיתוֹ בְּקָרוֹב.
בִּמְהֵרָה, בִּמְהֵרָה, בְּיָמֵינוּ בְּקָרוֹב.
אֵל בְּנֵה, אֵל בְּנֵה, בְּנֵה בֵיתְךָ בְּקָרוֹב.

נוֹרָא הוּא, סַגִּיב הוּא, עִזּוּז הוּא,
פּוֹדֶה הוּא, צַדִּיק הוּא יִבְנֶה בֵּיתוֹ בְּקָרוֹב.
בִּמְהֵרָה, בִּמְהֵרָה, בְּיָמֵינוּ בְּקָרוֹב.
אֵל בְּנֵה, אֵל בְּנֵה, בְּנֵה בֵיתְךָ בְּקָרוֹב.

קָדוֹשׁ הוּא, רַחוּם הוּא, שַׁדַּי הוּא,
תַּקִּיף הוּא יִבְנֶה בֵּיתוֹ בְּקָרוֹב.
בִּמְהֵרָה, בִּמְהֵרָה, בְּיָמֵינוּ בְּקָרוֹב.
אֵל בְּנֵה, אֵל בְּנֵה, בְּנֵה בֵיתְךָ בְּקָרוֹב.

God's own grace on this place, God will build the Temple soon:
Quickly, while we're living, soon.
Build the Temple soon.

God, the wisdom and the legend, God will build the Temple soon:
Quickly, while we're living, soon.
Build the Temple soon.

God who made the universe, God will build the Temple soon:
Quickly, while we're living, soon.
Build the Temple soon.

God makes meaning, law, redemption,
God will build the Temple soon:
Quickly, while we're living, soon.
Build the Temple soon.

God keep us on the side of mercy, God will build the Temple soon:
Quickly, while we're living, soon. Build the Temple soon.

אֶחָד מִי יוֹדֵעַ, אֶחָד אֲנִי יוֹדֵעַ.

אֶחָד אֱלֹהֵינוּ שֶׁבַּשָּׁמַיִם וּבָאָרֶץ:

שְׁנַיִם מִי יוֹדֵעַ, שְׁנַיִם אֲנִי יוֹדֵעַ.
שְׁנֵי לֻחוֹת הַבְּרִית. אֶחָד אֱלֹהֵינוּ שֶׁבַּשָּׁמַיִם וּבָאָרֶץ:

שְׁלֹשָׁה מִי יוֹדֵעַ, שְׁלֹשָׁה אֲנִי יוֹדֵעַ.
שְׁלֹשָׁה אָבוֹת, שְׁנֵי לֻחוֹת הַבְּרִית,
אֶחָד אֱלֹהֵינוּ שֶׁבַּשָּׁמַיִם וּבָאָרֶץ:

אַרְבַּע מִי יוֹדֵעַ, אַרְבַּע אֲנִי יוֹדֵעַ.
אַרְבַּע אִמָּהוֹת, שְׁלֹשָׁה אָבוֹת, שְׁנֵי לֻחוֹת הַבְּרִית,
אֶחָד אֱלֹהֵינוּ שֶׁבַּשָּׁמַיִם וּבָאָרֶץ:

חֲמִשָּׁה מִי יוֹדֵעַ, חֲמִשָּׁה אֲנִי יוֹדֵעַ.
חֲמִשָּׁה חוּמְשֵׁי תוֹרָה, אַרְבַּע אִמָּהוֹת, שְׁלֹשָׁה אָבוֹת, שְׁנֵי לֻחוֹת הַבְּרִית, אֶחָד אֱלֹהֵינוּ שֶׁבַּשָּׁמַיִם וּבָאָרֶץ:

שִׁשָּׁה מִי יוֹדֵעַ, שִׁשָּׁה אֲנִי יוֹדֵעַ.
שִׁשָּׁה סִדְרֵי מִשְׁנָה, חֲמִשָּׁה חוּמְשֵׁי תוֹרָה,
אַרְבַּע אִמָּהוֹת, שְׁלֹשָׁה אָבוֹת, שְׁנֵי לֻחוֹת הַבְּרִית,
אֶחָד אֱלֹהֵינוּ שֶׁבַּשָּׁמַיִם וּבָאָרֶץ:

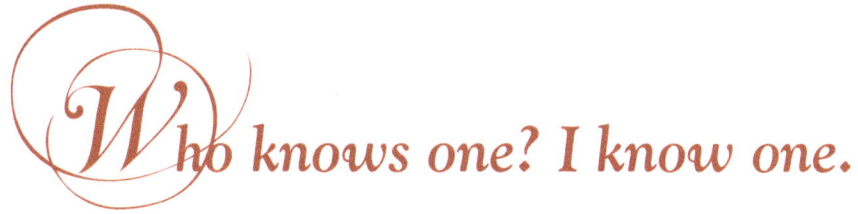 Who knows one? I know one.

One is God of heaven and earth.

Who knows two? I know two.
Two stone tablets of the Law;
One is God of heaven and earth.

Who knows three? I know three:
Three Patriarchs; Two stone tablets of the Law;
One is God of heaven and earth.

Who knows four? I know four:
Four Matriarchs; Three Patriarchs; Two stone tablets of the Law; One is God of heaven and earth.

Who knows five? I know five:
Five the Books of Torah; Four Matriarchs;
Three Patriarchs; Two stone tablets of the Law;
One is God of heaven and earth.

Who knows six? I know six:
Six sections of Mishnah; Five the Books of Torah; Four Matriarchs; Three Patriarchs; Two stone tablets of the Law; One is God of heaven and earth.

שִׁבְעָה מִי יוֹדֵעַ, שִׁבְעָה אֲנִי יוֹדֵעַ.
שִׁבְעָה יְמֵי שַׁבַּתָּא, שִׁשָּׁה סִדְרֵי מִשְׁנָה, חֲמִשָּׁה חוּמְשֵׁי תוֹרָה, אַרְבַּע אִמָּהוֹת, שְׁלֹשָׁה אָבוֹת, שְׁנֵי לֻחוֹת הַבְּרִית, אֶחָד אֱלֹהֵינוּ שֶׁבַּשָּׁמַיִם וּבָאָרֶץ:

שְׁמוֹנָה מִי יוֹדֵעַ, שְׁמוֹנָה אֲנִי יוֹדֵעַ.
שְׁמוֹנָה יְמֵי מִילָה, שִׁבְעָה יְמֵי שַׁבַּתָּא, שִׁשָּׁה סִדְרֵי מִשְׁנָה, חֲמִשָּׁה חוּמְשֵׁי תוֹרָה, אַרְבַּע אִמָּהוֹת, שְׁלֹשָׁה אָבוֹת, שְׁנֵי לֻחוֹת הַבְּרִית, אֶחָד אֱלֹהֵינוּ שֶׁבַּשָּׁמַיִם וּבָאָרֶץ:

תִּשְׁעָה מִי יוֹדֵעַ, תִּשְׁעָה אֲנִי יוֹדֵעַ.
תִּשְׁעָה יַרְחֵי לֵדָה, שְׁמוֹנָה יְמֵי מִילָה, שִׁבְעָה יְמֵי שַׁבַּתָּא, שִׁשָּׁה סִדְרֵי מִשְׁנָה, חֲמִשָּׁה חוּמְשֵׁי תוֹרָה, אַרְבַּע אִמָּהוֹת, שְׁלֹשָׁה אָבוֹת, שְׁנֵי לֻחוֹת הַבְּרִית, אֶחָד אֱלֹהֵינוּ שֶׁבַּשָּׁמַיִם וּבָאָרֶץ:

עֲשָׂרָה מִי יוֹדֵעַ, עֲשָׂרָה אֲנִי יוֹדֵעַ.
עֲשָׂרָה דִבְּרַיָּא, תִּשְׁעָה יַרְחֵי לֵדָה, שְׁמוֹנָה יְמֵי מִילָה, שִׁבְעָה יְמֵי שַׁבַּתָּא, שִׁשָּׁה סִדְרֵי מִשְׁנָה, חֲמִשָּׁה חוּמְשֵׁי תוֹרָה, אַרְבַּע אִמָּהוֹת, שְׁלֹשָׁה אָבוֹת, שְׁנֵי לֻחוֹת הַבְּרִית, אֶחָד אֱלֹהֵינוּ שֶׁבַּשָּׁמַיִם וּבָאָרֶץ:

Who knows seven? I know seven:
Seven days of the week; Six sections of Mishnah; Five the Books of Torah; Four Matriarchs; Three Patriarchs; Two stone tablets of the Law; One is God of heaven and earth.

Who knows eight? I know eight:
Eight days before the *brit milah*; Seven days of the week; Six sections of Mishnah; Five the Books of Torah; Four Matriarchs; Three Patriarchs; Two stone tablets of the Law; One is God of heaven and earth.

Who knows nine? I know nine:
Nine months of pregnancy; Eight days before the *brit milah*; Seven days of the week; Six sections of Mishnah; Five the Books of Torah; Four Matriarchs; Three Patriarchs; Two stone tablets of the Law; One is God of heaven and earth.

Who knows ten? I know ten:
Ten, the Ten Commandments; Nine months of pregnancy; Eight days before the *brit milah*; Seven days of the week; Six sections of Mishnah; Five the Books of Torah; Four Matriarchs; Three Patriarchs; Two stone tablets of the Law; One is God of heaven and earth.

אַחַד עָשָׂר מִי יוֹדֵעַ, אַחַד עָשָׂר אֲנִי יוֹדֵעַ.
אַחַד עָשָׂר כּוֹכְבַיָּא, עֲשָׂרָה דִבְּרַיָּא, תִּשְׁעָה יַרְחֵי לֵדָה, שְׁמוֹנָה יְמֵי מִילָה, שִׁבְעָה יְמֵי שַׁבַּתָּא, שִׁשָּׁה סִדְרֵי מִשְׁנָה, חֲמִשָּׁה חוּמְשֵׁי תוֹרָה, אַרְבַּע אִמָהוֹת, שְׁלֹשָׁה אָבוֹת, שְׁנֵי לֻחוֹת הַבְּרִית, אֶחָד אֱלֹהֵינוּ שֶׁבַּשָּׁמַיִם וּבָאָרֶץ:

שְׁנֵים עָשָׂר מִי יוֹדֵעַ, שְׁנֵים עָשָׂר אֲנִי יוֹדֵעַ.
שְׁנֵים עָשָׂר שִׁבְטַיָּא, אַחַד עָשָׂר כּוֹכְבַיָּא, עֲשָׂרָה דִבְּרַיָּא, תִּשְׁעָה יַרְחֵי לֵדָה, שְׁמוֹנָה יְמֵי מִילָה, שִׁבְעָה יְמֵי שַׁבַּתָּא, שִׁשָּׁה סִדְרֵי מִשְׁנָה, חֲמִשָּׁה חוּמְשֵׁי תוֹרָה, אַרְבַּע אִמָהוֹת, שְׁלֹשָׁה אָבוֹת, שְׁנֵי לֻחוֹת הַבְּרִית, אֶחָד אֱלֹהֵינוּ שֶׁבַּשָּׁמַיִם וּבָאָרֶץ:

שְׁלֹשָׁה עָשָׂר מִי יוֹדֵעַ, שְׁלֹשָׁה עָשָׂר אֲנִי יוֹדֵעַ.
שְׁלֹשָׁה עָשָׂר מִדַיָּא. שְׁנֵים עָשָׂר שִׁבְטַיָּא, אַחַד עָשָׂר כּוֹכְבַיָּא, עֲשָׂרָה דִבְּרַיָּא, תִּשְׁעָה יַרְחֵי לֵדָה, שְׁמוֹנָה יְמֵי מִילָה, שִׁבְעָה יְמֵי שַׁבַּתָּא, שִׁשָּׁה סִדְרֵי מִשְׁנָה, חֲמִשָּׁה חוּמְשֵׁי תוֹרָה, אַרְבַּע אִמָהוֹת, שְׁלֹשָׁה אָבוֹת, שְׁנֵי לֻחוֹת הַבְּרִית, אֶחָד אֱלֹהֵינוּ שֶׁבַּשָּׁמַיִם וּבָאָרֶץ:

Who knows eleven? I know eleven:
Eleven stars in Joseph's dream; Ten, the Ten Commandments; Nine months of pregnancy; Eight days before the *brit milah*; Seven days of the week; Six sections of Mishnah; Five the Books of Torah; Four Matriarchs; Three Patriarchs; Two stone tablets of the Law; One is God of heaven and earth.

Who knows twelve? I know twelve:
Twelve tribes of Israel; Eleven stars in Joseph's dream; Ten, the Ten Commandments; Nine months of pregnancy; Eight days before the *brit milah*; Seven days of the week; Six sections of Mishnah; Five the Books of Torah; Four Matriarchs; Three Patriarchs; Two stone tablets of the Law; One is God of heaven and earth.

Who knows thirteen? I know thirteen:
Thirteen attributes of God; Twelve tribes of Israel; Eleven stars in Joseph's dream; Ten, the Ten Commandments; Nine months of pregnancy; Eight days before the *brit milah*; Seven days of the week; Six sections of Mishnah; Five the Books of Torah; Four Matriarchs; Three Patriarchs; Two stone tablets of the Law; One is God of heaven and earth.

חַד גַּדְיָא, חַד גַּדְיָא

דְּזַבִּין אַבָּא בִּתְרֵי זוּזֵי, חַד גַּדְיָא, חַד גַּדְיָא.

וְאָתָא שׁוּנְרָא וְאָכְלָה לְגַדְיָא,
דְּזַבִּין אַבָּא בִּתְרֵי זוּזֵי, חַד גַּדְיָא, חַד גַּדְיָא.

וְאָתָא כַלְבָּא וְנָשַׁךְ לְשׁוּנְרָא, דְּאָכְלָה לְגַדְיָא,
דְּזַבִּין אַבָּא בִּתְרֵי זוּזֵי, חַד גַּדְיָא, חַד גַּדְיָא.

וְאָתָא חוּטְרָא וְהִכָּה לְכַלְבָּא, דְּנָשַׁךְ לְשׁוּנְרָא, דְּאָכְלָה לְגַדְיָא, דְּזַבִּין אַבָּא בִּתְרֵי זוּזֵי, חַד גַּדְיָא, חַד גַּדְיָא.

וְאָתָא נוּרָא וְשָׂרַף לְחוּטְרָא, דְּהִכָּה לְכַלְבָּא, דְּנָשַׁךְ לְשׁוּנְרָא, דְּאָכְלָה לְגַדְיָא,
דְּזַבִּין אַבָּא בִּתְרֵי זוּזֵי, חַד גַּדְיָא, חַד גַּדְיָא.

וְאָתָא מַיָּא וְכָבָה לְנוּרָא, דְּשָׂרַף לְחוּטְרָא, דְּהִכָּה לְכַלְבָּא, דְּנָשַׁךְ לְשׁוּנְרָא, דְּאָכְלָה לְגַדְיָא,
דְּזַבִּין אַבָּא בִּתְרֵי זוּזֵי, חַד גַּדְיָא, חַד גַּדְיָא.

וְאָתָא תוֹרָא וְשָׁתָה לְמַיָּא, דְּכָבָה לְנוּרָא, דְּשָׂרַף לְחוּטְרָא, דְּהִכָּה לְכַלְבָּא, דְּנָשַׁךְ לְשׁוּנְרָא, דְּאָכְלָה לְגַדְיָא,
דְּזַבִּין אַבָּא בִּתְרֵי זוּזֵי, חַד גַּדְיָא, חַד גַּדְיָא.

Had Gadya

**One kid, One little kid.
My father bought for two zuzim.**

A cat passed by and ate the kid,
One kid, One little kid. My father bought for two zuzim.

A dog arrived and bit the cat, that ate the kid,
One kid, One little kid. My father bought for two zuzim.

A heavy stick then beat the dog that bit the cat,
that ate the kid,
One kid, One little kid. My father bought for two zuzim.

A fire burned the heavy stick that beat the dog, that bit
the cat, that ate the kid,
One kid, One little kid. My father bought for two zuzim.

Water put the fire out that burned the stick,
that beat the dog that bit the cat, that ate the kid,
One kid, One little kid. My father bought for two zuzim.

An ox drank all that water that doused the fire,
that burned the stick that beat the dog
that bit the cat, that ate the kid,
One kid, One little kid. My father bought for two zuzim.

וְאָתָא הַשׁוֹחֵט וְשָׁחַט לְתוֹרָא, דְּשָׁתָה לְמַיָּא, דְּכָבָה
לְנוּרָא, דְּשָׂרַף לְחוּטְרָא, דְּהִכָּה לְכַלְבָּא,
דְּנָשַׁךְ לְשׁוּנְרָא, דְּאָכְלָה לְגַדְיָא,
דְּזַבִּין אַבָּא בִּתְרֵי זוּזֵי, חַד גַּדְיָא, חַד גַּדְיָא.

וְאָתָא מַלְאַךְ הַמָּוֶת וְשָׁחַט לְשׁוֹחֵט, דְּשָׁחַט לְתוֹרָא,
דְּשָׁתָה לְמַיָּא, דְּכָבָה לְנוּרָא, דְּשָׂרַף לְחוּטְרָא, דְּהִכָּה
לְכַלְבָּא, דְּנָשַׁךְ לְשׁוּנְרָא, דְּאָכְלָה לְגַדְיָא,
דְּזַבִּין אַבָּא בִּתְרֵי זוּזֵי, חַד גַּדְיָא, חַד גַּדְיָא.

וְאָתָא הַקָּדוֹשׁ בָּרוּךְ הוּא וְשָׁחַט לְמַלְאַךְ הַמָּוֶת,
דְּשָׁחַט לְשׁוֹחֵט, דְּשָׁחַט לְתוֹרָא, דְּשָׁתָה לְמַיָּא, דְּכָבָה
לְנוּרָא, דְּשָׂרַף לְחוּטְרָא, דְּהִכָּה לְכַלְבָּא, דְּנָשַׁךְ לְשׁוּנְרָא,
דְּאָכְלָה לְגַדְיָא, דְּזַבִּין אַבָּא בִּתְרֵי זוּזֵי, חַד גַּדְיָא, חַד גַּדְיָא.

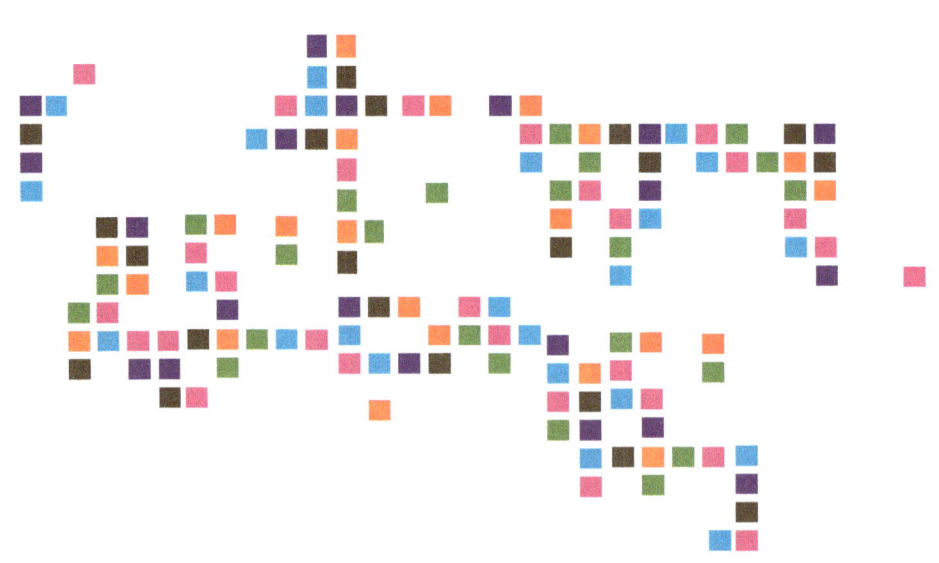

A butcher slaughtered the same ox that drank the water, that doused the fire that burned the stick that beat the dog that bit the cat, that ate the kid,
One kid, One little kid. My father bought for two zuzim.

The Angel of Death took off butcher who slaughtered the ox, that drank the water that doused the fire that burned the stick, that beat the dog that bit the cat,
That ate the kid.
One kid, One little kid. My father bought for two zuzim.

Then the Holy One Blessed be He killed the Angel of Death, who took off the butcher, who slaughtered the ox that drank the water, that doused the fire that burned the stick, that beat the dog that bit the cat, that ate the kid,
One kid, One little kid. My father bought for two zuzim.

Acknowledgements, Permissions & Notes

Holiday of Freedom: dom: Rabbi Joseph Radinsky, *Book VII*. With permission of the author.

The Warsaw Ghetto Uprising: Binem Heller, *"In Warshaver Ghetto is Hodesh Nisan,"* by Philip Goodman. Published by the Jewish Publication Society. With permission of the publisher.

What if Tomorrow There is No Bread? *A Night to Remember* by Noam Zion. Retold by Bina Talitman. With permission of the author.

Passover of 1945: Binyomin Orenshtayn, *"Passover Under the Rule of Hitlerite Tyranny,"* From a Ruined Garden: the Memorial Books of Polish Jewry, Indiana Univrsity Press. 1998. With permission of the publisher.

The Road Taken: Rabbi Avi Shafran, excerpt from The Road Taken, Project Genesis, Torah.org. With permission of the publisher.

Israel as the Center of the World: Anne Bayefsky. *Israel @60*. Copyright 2008 by National Review Inc., reprinted with permission

The Pesach Sacrifice: Its Positive and Negative Commandments; Rabbi S.Y. Zevin. *The Festivals in Halachah*, 1969, p. 25. Reprinted with permission from ArtScroll / Mesorah Publications Ltd.

Bread as a Symbol of Transformation. Peter Reinhart. *Peter Reinhart on Bread*, 2008. Ted.com

Beginnings of Acknowledgement. Rabbi Irving M Bunim. *Ever Since Sinai*. Feldheim Publishers, 1977. p. 137. With permission of Rabbi Bunim's family.

The Jewish Mayflower. David Ben Gurian. Excerpt of a speech delivered to the United Nations, 1947.

Beginnings are Difficult. Rabbi Eliyahu Hoffmann. Excerpt from the essay *Growth in Torah, Getting over the Baby Steps*, Project Genesis, Torah.org. With permission of the publisher.

All Questions are Permitted: Reprinted with the permission of Simon & Schuster, Inc. from A *Passover Haggadah* as commented upon by Elie Wiesel. Copyright 1993 Elirion Associates, Inc., and Mark Podwal.

Pesach Rules: Rabbi Joseph Radinsky, *Book VII*. With permission of the author.

The Rambam on Freedom. Rabbi Moses Maimonides (1135-1204) Mishna Torah, Laws on Repentance, chapter 5.

Gratitude. Rabbi Mordechai Torczyner. Excerpt from *The Rebbetzin's Husband*. rechovot.blogspot.com. With permission of the author.

The Wolves Within. Anonymous. Believed to be a native American (Cherokee) folk story.

A Discourse on Free Will. Jonathon Rosenblum. Jewish Media Resources. With permission of the author.

Imprisoned in Our Time. Excerpt from biography, *Gilad Shalit*, Haaretz, Israel. With permission of the publisher.

Power of Community. Emuna Braverman. *The Power of Community*, Aish.com. With permission of the publisher.

To Be Inclusive not Exclusive. Rabbi Shlomo Riskin. Excerpt from the essay *Parshat Metzora*, 2003. With permission of the author.

Approach #1. Rabbi Marc Angel. *Losing the Rat Race and Winning at Life*. Urim Publications, 2005, p. 17. With permission of the author.

The Value of Trying. Yakov Fogelman. Torah Outreach Project. With permission of the author.

Free at Last. Based on reports from the Dallas Morning News and The Huffington Post, January 2011.

Join a Group. Rabbi Boruch Leff. Excerpted from *Vayakhel, The Power of Community*, 2002. Aish.com. With permission of the author.

Momentum. Rabbi Mordechai Kamenetzky. Excerpted from *Vaera; Lost in Egypt*. 1996. Project Genesis. Torah.org. With permission from the publisher.

A Glass Half Full: *A Code of Jewish Ethics, Volume 1: You Shall be Holy* by Rabbi Joseph Telushkin, copyright 2006 by Rabbi Joseph Telushkin. Used by permission of Bell Tower, a division of Random House, Inc. Any third party use of this material, outside of this publication, is prohibited. Interested parties must apply directly to Random House, Inc. for permission.

Zionism as Progress. Winston Churchill. This is an excerpt of a reply from Mr. Churchill to an Arab delegation in Jerusalem, 1821.

Recognizing the Good. Alan Morinis, PHD. Jewishpathways.com. With permission from the author.

Jewish Unity- Unity Does Not Mean Conformity. Riva Pomerantz. Excerpt from *Unified Jews Theory*, 2004. Aish.com, An award winning website. With permission of the author and publisher.

Yearning for Return. Rabbi David Wolpe. The Jewish Week, May 21, 2010. With permission of the author.

Invictus. William Ernest Henley. *Book of Verses*, 1875

I Must Become We. Rabbi Shlomo Riskin. *Shabbat Hagadol*, 2001. With permission of the author.

Overcoming Suffering. Reprinted with the permission of Simon & Schuster, Inc. from A *Passover Haggadah* as commented upon by Elie Wiesel. Copyright 1993 Elirion Associates, Inc., and Mark Podwal.

Neighborhood Bully. Bob Dylan. Special Rider Music, Sony. 1983

Transforming the Past. David Silberman. Based in part from a sermon by Rabbi Barry Gelman

True Gratitude. Rabbi Adam Lieberman. *Gratitude Has No Expiration Date*. Aish.com, 2006. With permission of the publisher.

Obstacles to Transformation Can be Overcome. Rabbi Mordechai Kamenetzky, Project Genesis, Torah.org. With permission from the publisher.

Concepts of Freedom Approach #2, Rabbi Shmuley Boteach. Excerpted from: *Passover and the Liberation from Typological Slavery*, 2005. With permission from the author.

The Jewish Gratitude Blessing form Aaron Z., Courtesy of Jewish Alcoholics and Chemically Dependent Persons and Significant Others, New York City, NY., 2011.

Connecting to Community, Steve Israel, Connecting to Community, Jewish Agency for Israel

Da'yenu, Rabbi Menachem Leibtag, *Da'yenu, A Shir for Pesach and Yom Atzmaut*, The Tanach Study Center. With permission of the author.

Concepts of Freedom #3, Rabbi Pinchas Kantrowitz, *Let Freedom Reign*, Ohr Somayach Institutions www.ohr.edu. With permission of the author.

The Hidden Hand That Had Given, President Abraham Lincoln, proclamation appointing a National Fast Day, March 30, 1863. (President Lincoln designated April 30 of that year to be a national day of prayer. Many presidents since then have proclaimed a national day of prayer and Congress ratified it as an actual law. Not every president has embraced this day and there are legal challenges to it as of this writing)

Achdut - Jewish Unity, Rabbi Adin Steinsaltz, Excerpt from a lecture Achdut - Jewish Unity, Aleph Society., 1999.

The Value of Appreciation, Rabbi Adin Steinsaltz, *Thankful for Thanksgiving*, Aleph Society, 2002

Internal Transformation - *Searching for Chametz Within*, Rabbi Yehudah Prero, Searching for Chametz Within, Project Genesis, Torah.org. With permission of the publisher.

The Stories of Six Survivors, The Stories of Six Survivors Who Have Rebuilt Their Lives in Israel, by the staff of the Jerusalem Post, 2008.

Concepts in Freedom #4, Noam Zion, *Freedom is the Ability to Conceive of Alternative Possibilities*, Shalom Hartman Institute, 2008. With permission of the author.

Gratitude Should be Long Lasting: *A Code of Jewish Ethics, Volume 1: You Shall be Holy* by Rabbi Joseph Telushkin, copyright 2006 by Rabbi Joseph Telushkin. Used by permission of Bell Tower, a division of Random House, Inc. Any third party use of this material, outside of this publication, is prohibited. Interested parties must apply directly to Random House, Inc. for permission.

Slavery Around Us, Mordekhai Eliav, Ani Ma'amin, Mosad Harav Kook Publishing, 2006. With permission from the publisher.

Long Road to Israel, Excerpt from The *Letters of Jonathan Netanyahu, Self Portrait of a Hero*, Torah Outreach Program, 1998. With permission of the publisher. Jonathan Netanyahu, brother of the prime minister of Israel, Benjamin Netanyahu, was the sole casualty of the Israeli rescuers sent to Entebbe, Uganda, to rescue Jewish hostages in 1976.

Passover Transcends Generations, Rabbi Abraham Twersky, *Generation to Generation*, C.I.S. Publishers, 1985, p. 95. With permission from the publishers.

Freedom: A Choice of a Certain Action: Man's Search for Meaning, By Viktor E. Frankl, Copyright 1959, 1962, 1984, 1992 by Viktor E. Frankl, Reprinted by permission of Beacon Press, Boston.

Thanking God for Israel, Harav Yehuda Amital, except from *The Religious Significance of the State of Israel,* Yeshivat Har Etzion, 1997. With permission of the publisher.

Being Grateful Prior to a Loss: *A Code of Jewish Ethics, Volume 1: You Shall be Holy* by Rabbi Joseph Telushkin, copyright 2006 by Rabbi Joseph Telushkin. Used by permission of Bell Tower, a division of Random House, Inc. Any third party use of this material, outside of this publication, is prohibited. Interested parties must apply directly to Random House, Inc. for permission.

Paradox of Freedom, based on a lecture by Barry Schwartz entitled *The Paradox of Choice,* Ted.com. With permission of the publisher.

Redemption in an Instant: excerpt from *Schindler's List* by Thomas Keneally, Touchstone Publishing, 1993. With permission from the publisher.

Unity is Crucial When facing an Adversary: Dov Krulwich, *Harry Potter and Torah,* Lulu Publishing, 2007. With permission from the author.

Today We are Slaves: Irving J. Rosenbaum, *The Holocaust and Halakhah,* Mosad Harav Kook Publishers, 1976, p 99. With permission of the publisher.

Personal Change: excerpt from Rabbi Yissochar Frand, *Parshat Kedoshim,* Project Genesis, Torah.org. With permission of the publisher.

Korech: Restoring Jewish Unity: excerpt from Rabbi Shraga Simmons, *Dvar Tora Pesach* by Dovid Green et al, Genesis Project, Torah.org. With permission of the publisher.

Grateful Guests: *A Code of Jewish Ethics, Volume 1: You Shall be Holy* by Rabbi Joseph Telushkin, copyright 2006 by Rabbi Joseph Telushkin. Used by permission of Bell Tower, a division of Random House, Inc. Any third party use of this material, outside of this publication, is prohibited. Interested parties must apply directly to Random House, Inc. for permission.

Songs of Dreamers: Natan Sharansky, *Fear No Evil,* Random House New York, 1988, p. 410. With permission of the publisher. Natan Sharansky was imprisoned by the Soviet Union under the false charge of espionage. He was released after eleven years in 1986.

For One Brief Moment the Jew Stood Tall: Deborah E. Lipstadt, author of *History on Trial: My day in Court with David Irving.* This work is her account of her successful defense of a libel suit by a Holocaust denier, David Irving. With permission of the author.

Israel the Realized Dream: Gershon Winer, Excerpt from *The Founding Fathers of Israel,* Bloch Publishing, 2001. With permission of the publisher.

Exodus and Aliya: Excerpted from *The Palyam and Aliya Bet Website*. With permission of the publisher.

Passover - A Time for Reflection and Change. Rabbi Jerachmiel Danziger, *Yismach Yisrael Commentary on the Haggadah*, paraphrased by Rabbi Mark Greenspan, Torah Table Talk: When Does the New Year Begin?, Parshat Vayakhel. With permission of Rabbi Greenspan.

Appreciating Others and Being Appreciated: Excerpted from the teachings of Rabbi Yochanan Zweig, Talmudic University, Miami Florida.

It's About Continuity: Rabbi Berel Wein, *Jewish Amnesia*, Aish.com. With permission of the author. © The Destiny Foundation/ Rabbi Berel Wein- Jewish historian, author and international lecturer offers a complete selection of CDs, MP3, audio tapes, video, DVDs, and books on Jewish history at www.rabbiwein.com.

Israel the Destination: Arie Comey, translated by Yvonne Vador. Israel. Selected Readings for Independence Day, 1998, Israel Ministry of foreign Affairs.

Past and Present: Arnold Eisen, quoted from *The Jewish Holidays* by Michael Stassfeld, Harper Collins, 2011. With permission from the publishers

I would like to gratefully acknowledge:

the assistance of Sorelle Weinstein of Flowingpens.com for her editing prowess

and

the contributions of Emuna Carmel for her graphic art and typesetting skills